DECK and BOARDWALK DESIGN ESSENTIALS

EDGAR (TED) STUBBERSFIELD

With guest contributor

RALPH BAILEY

Copyright © 2012 Rachel Stubbersfield
All rights reserved.
ISBN: 0-9873994-1-1
ISBN-13: 978-0-9873994-1-0

About the Author

Ted Stubbersfield was born in the small Queensland town of Gatton in 1950. After studying to be a pastor in Brisbane and the UK he returned to the family business, Gatton Sawmilling Co. A fair question would be, can anything good come out of Gatton? Well, Gatton was the home of a Governor General of Australia (William Vanneck 1938). It is also the home of the best and most innovative hardwood producer in Australia, Outdoor Structures Australia (OSA).

The family had been involved in sawmilling and building for about 140 years and a lot of knowledge has passed through the generations. In 1985 we ventured into the footbridge market (almost by accident) and then followed public landscaping. Initially we just did as we were told by consultants who knew very little about timber. In about 1988 Ted decided he would come to know the medium he was working with far better than any of his competitors and most of the professionals who used his products.

Ted realised that there were no useful standards and guides for designing and building weather exposed timber structures such as boardwalks. That led in 1997 to his first formal research project on boardwalk design, engineering supply and construction. Over the years there followed a complete set of guides. These allowed professionals to design timber structures of exceptional beauty and durability. Typically, everybody wants to re-invent the wheel and the guides were usually ignored. Invariably, the same mistakes keep being made over and over. This little book is an attempt to remedy this.

In 2012, the time came to close the manufacturing arm of OSA and to take on a less stressful lifestyle. Ted plans to put in writing much of what he has learnt so the industry does not have to relearn it. This book is the second in a series of Timber Design Files that are intended to allow designers avoid the pitfalls of common but often bad practice and Standards that are very inadequate and engender a false sense of security.

Acknowledgements

If you find the content of this book helpful it is because I listened to and learned from others that knew more than me. I want to acknowledge their years of assistance.

James Pierce of James Pierce and Associates. James was our consulting engineer for over 22 years and undertook most of our formal research projects. He was behind those amazing OSA bridges.

Colin MacKenzie formerly of Tradac and later of Timber Queensland. Colin was a sounding board for many of our ideas and encouraged us as we attempted to set a course contrary to the direction of the tide.

Ralph Bailey of Guymer Bailey Architects. We have collaborated over the years and shared knowledge. Ralph, like me, has a love of timber and a passion for using it well. I have a profound respect for his abilities. Thank you for allowing me to include your analysis of different decking materials.

Contents

About the Author i
Acknowledgements ii
Introduction 3
Deck Design 101 5
   Why we design for Safety 5
   Why we Design for Durability 6
   The Assumptions 7
   Running the Decking Crossways 8
      Designing End Headstocks/Bearers 8
      Bolt End Clearance 9
      Vertical or Horizontal Bolts 10
      Determining Intermediate Headstock Positions 11
      Where it Starts to go Wrong. 12
      Joist Width 13
      Dampcourses 15
      Using Triple/Multigrips 16
      Bolted connections 18
      Bolt and Screw Type 18
      Getting the Lengthwise Joist layout Right 19
   Running the Decking Lengthways 23
      Why we Use Set length Decking 25
      Designing to a Module 25
Foundation issues 30
   Pier, Joist and Handrail Interaction 30
   Pile/Post Design 32
Decking Issues 33
   Ideal Decking Lengths 33
   Recycled or New Timber? 35
   Slip Resistance and Surface Finish 36
   Self Cleaning Decks 38
   How to Avoid Cupped Decking 40
   Decks and Ground Contact 41
   Shelling Out 42

- The Suitability of Pine for Decks/Boardwalks ... 44
- Take Care When Using or Specifying Kwila/Merbau ... 45
- Oiling Decking ... 46

Use of Different Joist Material ... 48
- Decking on Steel Joists ... 48
- Decking on LVL or Laminated Beams ... 50
- Decking on Fibre Composite Joists ... 52

Common Design Issues ... 53
- Changes of direction ... 53
  - Changes Up to 13 Degrees ... 53
  - Changes More Than 13 Degrees ... 55
  - Very Sharp Changes of Direction ... 55
- Decking Gaps ... 56
- Laying Deckwood on Concrete with Restricted Clearance ... 60

Notes on Hardware ... 62
- Alternative Fixings ... 62
- Volute Washers, a Useful Piece of Hardware ... 64
- Malthoid a Mixed Blessing ... 64
- Headstock Bolts Used with Natural Rounds ... 66

Some Case Histories ... 67
- Australian Examples ... 67
  - Specifications Should Mean Something ... 67
  - Calypso Bay Marina, as Good as it Gets ... 69
- International Examples ... 71
  - Noah's Ark in Hong Kong ... 71
  - Boardwalks for Singapore National Parks ... 73
  - Decks at Marinoa in Fukuoka, Japan ... 75
  - Dubai Yacht Club ... 76

Conclusion ... 78

Appendix A. Design Check List ... 79

Appendix B. Analysis of Alternate Decking material ... 85

Appendix C. A Suitable Decking Specification ... 89

Introduction

A few years ago I was walking over a boardwalk with my son-in-law and, not being able to help myself, began pointing out to him its design, supply and construction flaws. He had heard it all many times before and was probably a little bored with it and said, "But Ted, you have been saying this for years, why are we still seeing it?"

My answer was, "Yes, and it's getting worse!" From time to time I see a set of drawings that make me think that I will never see a design so poor again, only for it to be trumped by yet another. Timber structures fail on paper a long time before they fail in service. If the design is not right on paper, the resultant structure simply will not work the way you expect. Time and effort spent getting the details correct before a piece of timber is ordered will be rewarded by a structure that has a long life and ages gracefully whilst having little maintenance.

Fig. 1. "Down" is up and "Inside" is outside. Are these carpenters building your deck?

Perhaps I am getting cynical in my old age but, as you can gather; I am very disappointed by the level of professionalism at all levels by many of those involved with decks and boardwalks. This Guide is written to assist you as a designer rise above the rest by introducing certainty into your weather exposed timber projects. This will require far more detailing on the drawings than most designers are used to providing. But the beauty of CAD is that you only have to draw the details once and can reuse them many times. This level of detailing is necessary so you can tap the builder on the shoulder and say, "Fix it at your cost."

We used to pre-grade our boardwalk timber with "Inside" (away from the weather) and "Down" (to keep moisture out of any natural features). We doubted that most builders would take the care to assess the best way to place a member so we tried to assist them. When I saw the workmanship in Figure 1 with "Down" up and "Inside" out, I realised that pre-grading was a complete waste of time and never did it again. I continued pre-grading our decking for best side and, as the profile is not reversible, I thought it was not necessary to mark "This side up" until I actually saw someone lay Deckwood upside down! These builders may well be the lowest price tenderers that you have just contracted to build your deck and will be ready to cut as many corners as they can get away with. Beware!

Many of my readers will know that Outdoor Structures has four related publications, these being:

- Boardwalk Design Guide
- Boardwalk Construction Guide (Type 1 – Bedlog foundation)
- Boardwalk Construction Guide (Type 2 – Post and headstock foundation)
- Deckwood Selection Guide.

So why is there any need for a fifth publication? The original guides simply state best practice i.e. **how** to do certain things. Follow the system strictly to the letter and everything works well. But increasingly we were finding that people were picking and choosing what they wanted from the Guides. No one took up the phone and asked, "Can I use a 50 mm joist instead of 75 mm?" or "Can I use F11 KD hardwood instead of F17 unseasoned royal species?" I have had cases where the only thing the designer has picked up from the existing Guides is the use of an anti warp groove in the decking. This booklet deals with the "how" as well but its main emphasis is **why** we do certain things.

The outline adopted by this Guide is to work through the design issues involved in laying out a small deck measuring 12 x 3.6 m, first with decking running crosswise and then laying out for lengthwise decking. The following sections look in detail at various areas that cause complications such as decking gaps and changes of direction. This is followed by a section dealing with alternative construction materials. The guide then shows the application of these different sections with some good and bad case histories. As further assistance, a check list and a decking timber specification completes this Guide.

My *Timber Preservation Guide* contains masses of references; this book has few. The reason is that this book is the distilled experience that has taken a lifetime to learn.

Disclaimer
The information shown herein does not constitute a complete design so a Consulting Engineer with skills in both timber design and foundation systems should be engaged for the structural and foundation design.

Deck Design 101

Why we design for Safety

Fig. 2. Image from Archicentre press release.

Fig. 3. Image Courtesy of BSA

Frequently, a designer's/builder's frame of reference is "How cheaply can I build this deck?" But it is very wrong and I believe irresponsible. Decks do not come with a large sign that says "Demolish this deck in 20 years and start again." There should be such a sign when decks are built to a price.[1] The expected lifespan for these structures can be very long and, eventually, shortcuts always work their way to the surface.

Tragically, In November 2008, a roofed entertainment deck collapsed in Brisbane, killing one person. In that case, joists were cogged into the face of a bearer and skew nailed into place. After 90 years the nails finally rusted through. During a party, the bearer supporting a fully loaded deck bowed outwards and the joists spilled out of the bearer. In an instant, a mistake in construction made so long ago brought tragedy to the families involved. This is why it does matter if you use galvanised metal grips in places where the manufacturer says not to. This is why it does matter if you don't use timber of suitable

---

[1] Following a fatality in Yeppoon in 2011 the Rockhampton coroner recommended in September 2012 that state laws should be amended "to ensure mandatory inspections were undertaken on decks that were over 10 years old before a property was placed on the rental market, and that ongoing checks of decks were undertaken every three years thereafter". Hennessy, A.M. Coroner, *Inquest into the death of Isabella Wren Diefenbach*, Queensland Courts, 19 Sept. 2012, 59.

durability. This is why it does matter if you don't use the right bolt. And the list goes on.

How serious is the issue of poor deck design? Figures 2 and 3 show the terrible impact of the "she'll be right" attitude to design and the use of unsuitable timber and fixings. According to the Archicentre there could be as many as 8,000 of these potentially fatal balconies or decks throughout Australia.[2] Archicentre was not talking about sub-standard decks but life threatening decks!

We know that timber decks are perfect for the Australian lifestyle and while they look easy to design and build, there are several important design elements that need to be considered. I will now walk you through the basics of commercial deck design with some reference to domestic decks as well.

Why we Design for Durability

Fig. 4. Decking was the weak link.

The emphasis in this guide is on the subframe rather than the decking. Decking used to be the weak link, the area that failed first or at a similar time to the subframe. When we introduced Deckwood (and by Deckwood I do not mean the low grade imitations that were being passed off as Deckwood), the problems moved from the decking to the subframe. Designing the subframe for durability means ensuring that, when the deck eventually had to be replaced, it is all that has to be replaced. It is intended that the subframe, where most of the expense occurred during design and construction will be sound and can simply be re-decked. The deck shown in Figure 4 had completely failed and the subframe had also deteriorated and had to be replaced as well. The estimated cost for replacement after only 15 years was $1M for the timber alone. This should reinforce the point that a little extra expense at construction can bring major rewards in longevity and whole of life costs. A life expectancy of 15 years is appalling and can be far exceeded by taking care through designing for durability, not strength.

---

[2] "Archicentre's pre-purchase home inspection statistics show that approximately 6% of Australian homes have a timber balcony or deck and that about 2% of these (8000) are potentially fatal". Archicentre: *Architects Warn On Deadly Decks As People Gather For Xmas And New Year.* http://industry.newsarticles.net.au/Architecture/Architects-Warn-On-Deadly-Decks-As-People-Gather-For-Xmas-And-New-Year.htm. Date accessed 13 June 2012

Fig. 5. The first Deckwood sale changed our approach to decking.

When I went to photograph the very first order we sold of Deckwood, from a distance the deck in a rainforest setting looked absolutely stunning. When I got on the deck my heart sank. The joists were only 50 mm wide and they had all split from one end to the other. The screws were, and had to be, in a straight line. In a rainforest, splitting the joist is the worst thing that can happen as moisture enters the joist causing them to fail prematurely. That moment I realised that it was not enough to have an appropriate decking; it had to be a complete system of building. Our *Boardwalk Design Guide* was conceived that day. The system approach we adopted is explained as we proceed through Deck Design 101.

When I started down this path, practices, at times, could only be described as abysmal. Figure 6 which illustrates a very badly split narrow (38 mm) joist is an example,. Not surprisingly the boardwalk was very short lived. As we aimed to discover world's best practice we learnt that is a continually moving target and we have constantly had to "tweak" our recommendations in line with improved practices.

As I researched this guide I came to the conclusion that while our recommendations had been a vast improvement on what had gone on before, and had resulted in structures that performed well, there were still changes that could be made to extend the life of timber structures even further. Some of this better practice is hard to implement, simply because the necessary hardware is not available in every market and certainly not Australia at the time of writing.

Fig. 6. Badly split 38mm joist

The Assumptions

This part of the Guide looks at the steps involved in laying out a simple rectangular deck measuring 12 x 3.6 m. It doesn't get much easier but even here there is a lot that can impact on the subframe life and what you will be shown is generally more detailed than normal practice.

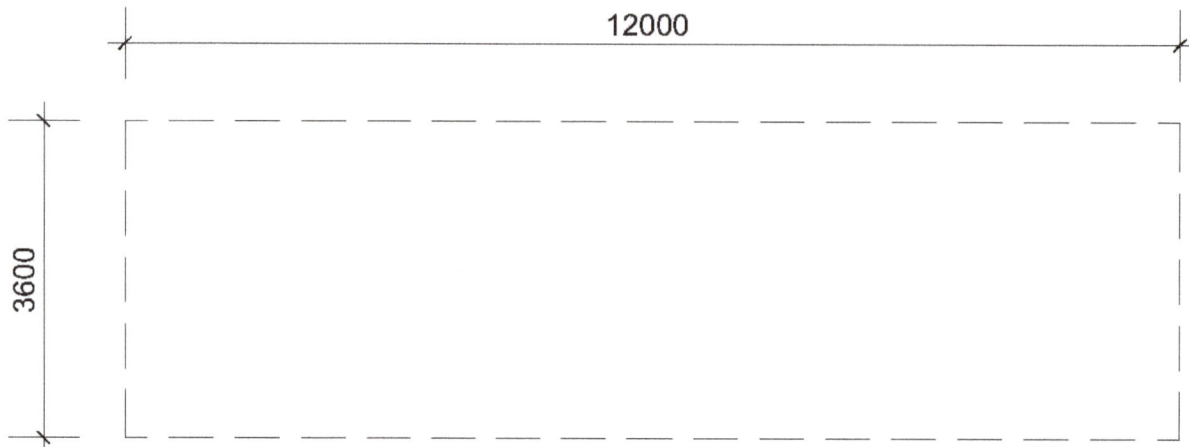

Fig. 7. Our starting point, a 12 x 3.6 m deck (plan view).

As always it is necessary to make some assumptions and these are:
- 120x35 Deckwood will be used and this will span 640 mm in a commercial deck (5 KPa, 4.5 KN)
- The boards will be face fixed
- As you should keep 90% of your decking order to 3.6 m or less to maximise sawmill recovery and improve quality, the deck boards will not exceed that length when being run lengthways
- When the boards run crosswise, lapped internal joists will be used.

Running the Decking Crossways

Designing End Headstocks/Bearers

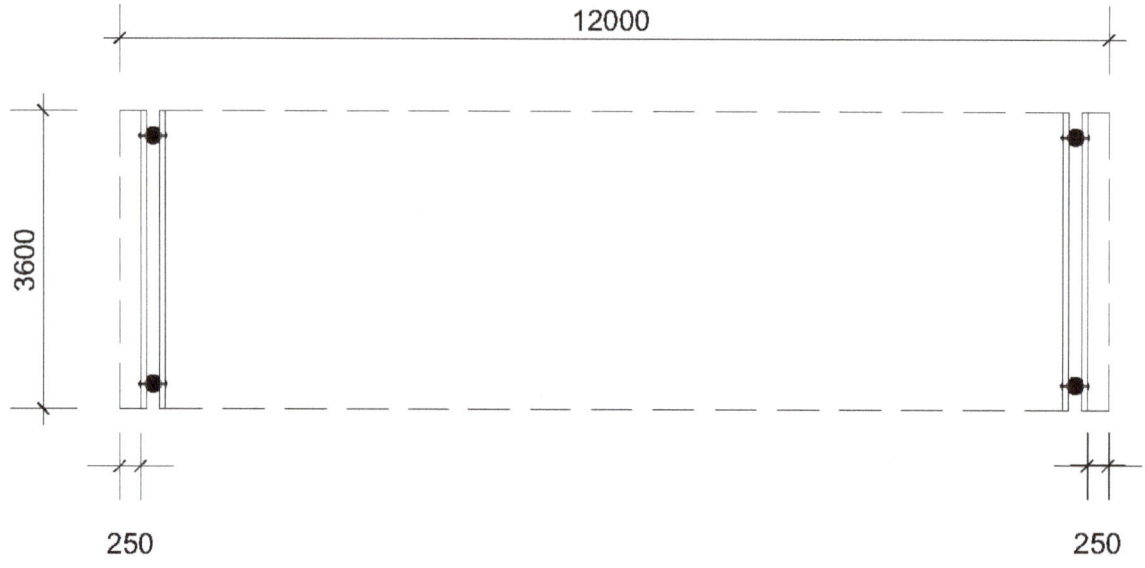

Fig. 8. Placing the headstocks.

We use a double headstock (a bridge building term, alternatively called the bearer) instead of a single piece. We see plans come out with sizes like 300x100 and I think, "Where are the forests now that will cut that in a suitable species and a suitable grade?" The forestry agreements have seen a big change in the size and quality of the logs and AS2080 has dropped its quality requirements so that a large piece of timber such as a 300x100 can be supplied with heart, i.e. the non-structural pith at the centre of the tree. This was never considered appropriate grading for hardwood.[3] A double headstock will keep the size down to something achievable from a sustainable Australian source and be supplied free of heart. There are also other advantages as we will see.

Fig. 9. Heart in material does not even make reasonable landscaping!

It is probably prudent to note on the drawings that "structural timber with a width of 150 mm is to be supplied *free of heart*". The phrase may need some adjustment to suit your particular job as it is impossible to cut a 200x150 mm kerb free of heart but you do not want a 250x100 mm joist with heart in. We took care of this automatically with our "Joistwood" but others pushed *AS2082 Timber-Hardwood-Visually stress graded for structural purposes* to its limits.

Bolt End Clearance

To keep the bolt end clearances for the joists I have set the outer edge of the headstock 250 mm from the extremity of the boardwalk. The actual distance varies from deck to deck depending on the handrail details. Bolt end clearances are very critical but can be overlooked. For Outdoor Structures this is fairly simple. The bolt should be 8 diameters from the end. We used a 12 mm bolt in our 150x75 mm joists so 12 mm x 8 diameters = 96 mm. We then add an extra 50 mm for weathering and you now have 150 mm. In this case the width (150 mm) equals the end clearance. It works the same for a 200 mm piece with a 20 mm bolt. Sometimes, however, it takes a lot of thought to be able to achieve this end clearance though.

---

[3] This is discussed in our guide *Grading Hardwood - Understanding AS2082*.

Vertical or Horizontal Bolts

Fig. 10. Horizontal bolting.

Fig. 11. Vertical Bolting.

Generally, deck and boardwalk construction has followed the practices adopted in timber bridge construction. The standard details for main roads bridges have basically remained unchanged for the last 100 years. This involves inserting bolts through the girders from the top right through the corbels and through bolting spiking planks to the girders from the top. This allows moisture to run down the bolts to the centre of the girders and cause the timber to fail prematurely. While there has been no change to Australian practice, modern overseas bridge construction has seen fasteners change from vertical to horizontal bolts and decking being secured from underneath. This makes complete sense.

Unfortunately, I have not found an ideal commercially available system (in Australia) for fastening decking from underneath. So, with the adoption of horizontal bolts and a bracket to fasten the joists to the bearers we are still left with screws on the face of the joists with all the problems that causes. We may not have advanced far at all. I also fear that vertical bolts are so deeply ingrained into the design and construction industry in Australia that it is not likely to change for a long time. So when you see reference in this guide to vertical bolts it is probably better to think horizontal bolts.

If you are going to use vertical bolts it is probably best to consider filling the countersunk top with a tar type product. When brackets are being used instead of vertical bolts, elongated holes will be required in the top of the bracket to allow the joist to shrink and still sit on the bearer.

Determining Intermediate Headstock Positions

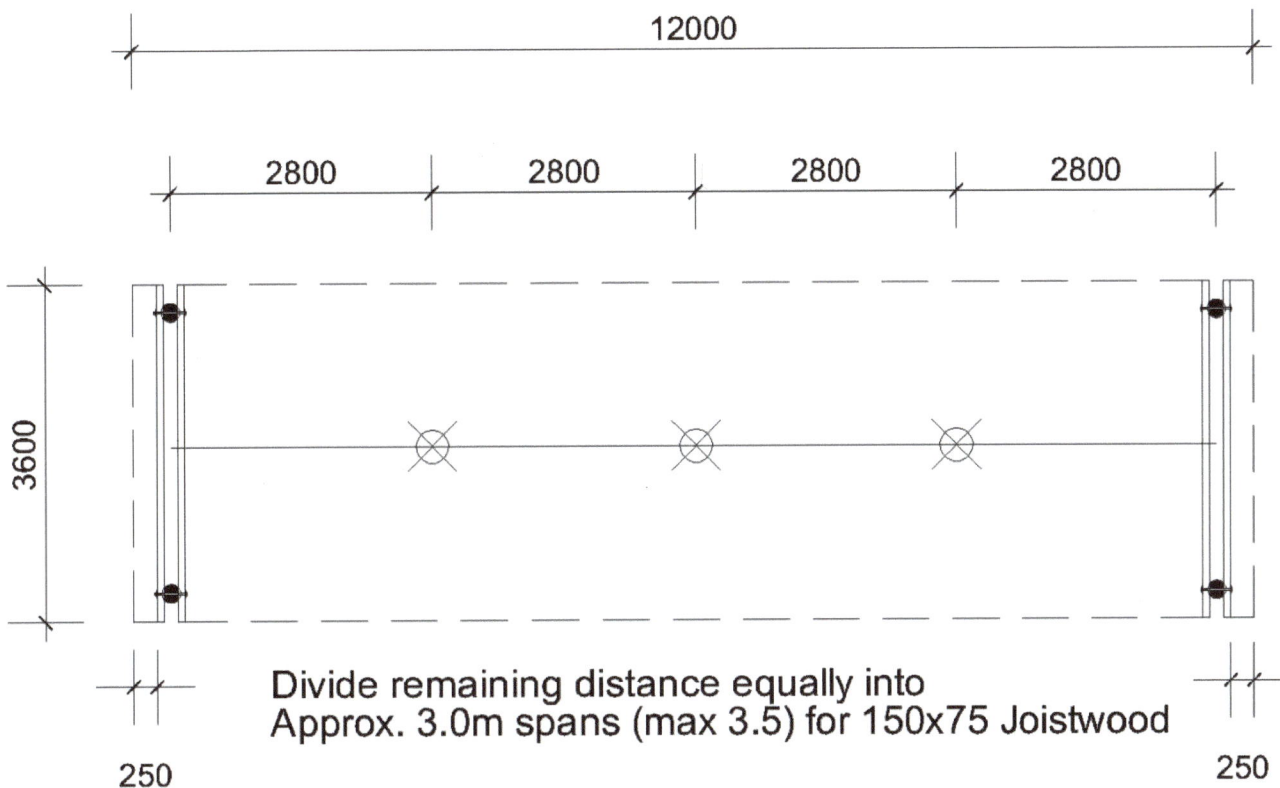

Fig. 12. Determine position of intermediate bearers.

To determine the positions of the other headstocks, divide the distance between the outside bearers into 3.0 m centres approximately but no more than 3.5 m. This will work for Outdoor Structures 150x75 mm Joistwood. Avoid using 175 or 200x75 mm as again you have a responsibility to use the limited resource wisely. The engineering in the *Deckwood Selection Guide* allows you to work within the limitations of the Forest Agreements without running afoul of the relaxations of included heart in AS2082.

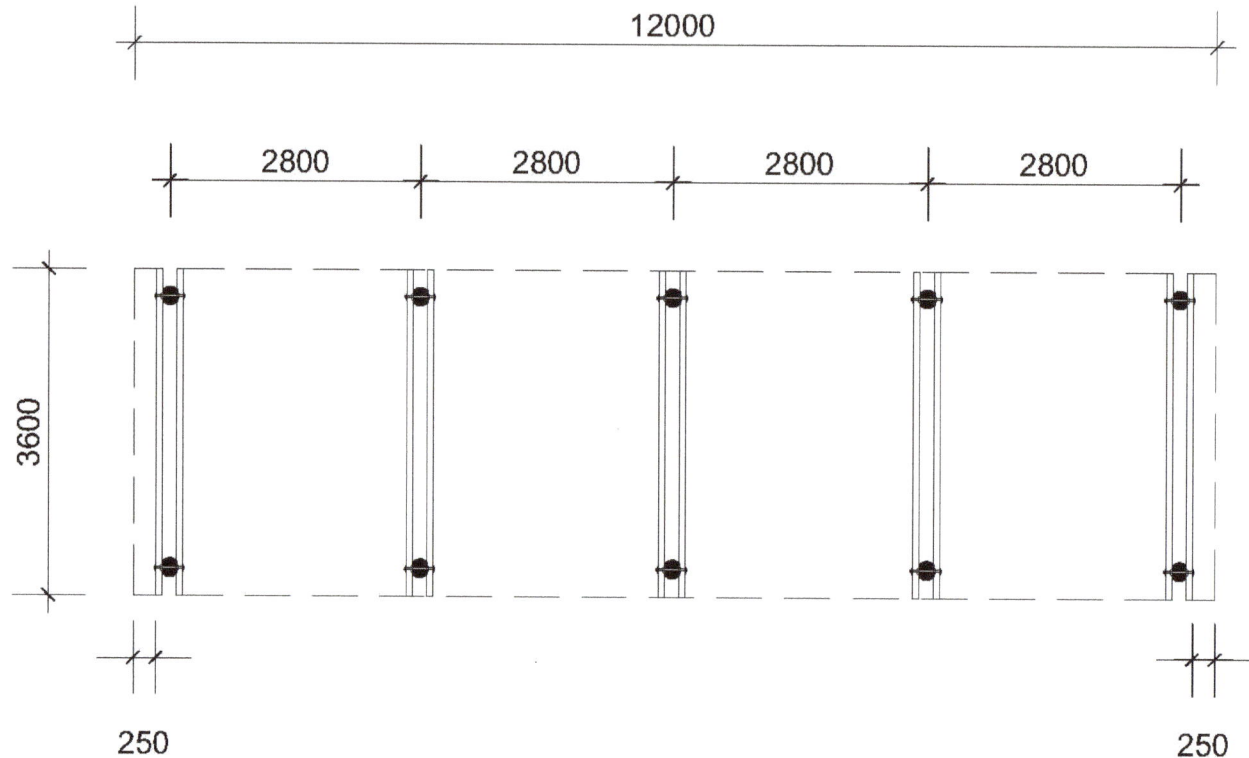

Fig. 13. Intermediate bearers drawn.

The next step is simply to copy the headstock sets to the nodes. You are now ready for the joists.

Where it Starts to go Wrong.

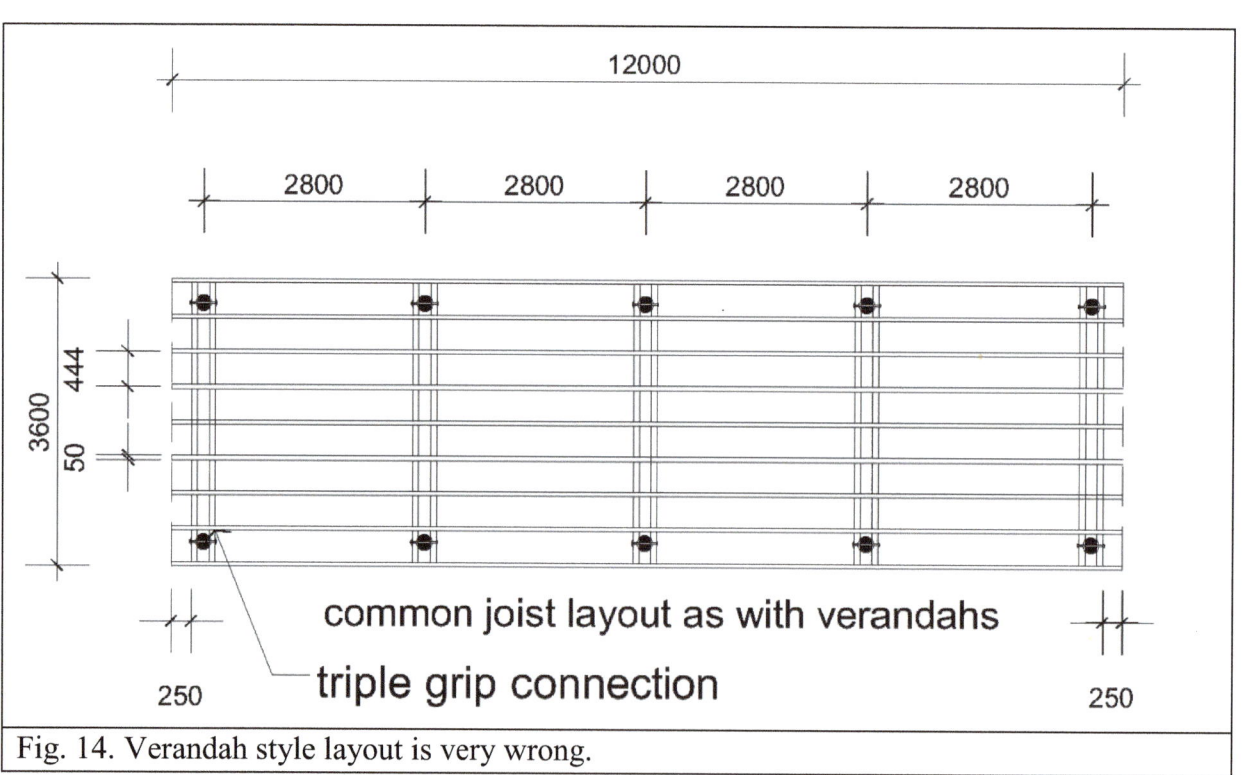

Fig. 14. Verandah style layout is very wrong.

It is at about this point that things tend to unravel. Designers can fail to understand the fundamental difference between a commercial deck and a domestic deck. Common mistakes are the use of narrow joists and triple grip fasteners. The problem associated with these products and correct material choice is explained as we proceed through Deck Design 101.

Joist Width

Often the joists are specified as 50 mm connected with triple grips and set at 450 mm centres. Sometimes, the outer joist is right at the edge. This may work for nailed 88x19 mm decking but is very unsatisfactory for heavy 35 mm or thicker decking with heavy 14# screws.

Fig. 15. Example of verandah style layout.

Fig. 16. Split 50mm joist on the same deck.

The failure of this traditional layout can be shown in the deck illustrated in Figures 15 and 16. There are two problems; the decking is too long and the joists are too thin. The best length for the decking is discussed later in this Guide. The design called up 50 mm joists which have now split from one end to the other. Some were split 5 mm before the builder left the site! The image of the joist in Figure 16 was taken about 12 months after completion. I spoke to someone in the company that built this deck and I was told, "We are not worried". I would not have slept at night as there was no way that this deck could be rectified apart from ripping it up, substructure and all, and starting again. If I had been the asset owner I would have insisted that it be repaired! Then the fight would begin about who is responsible.

| Fig. 17. Screw alignment on 50mm joist. | Fig. 18. Degrade of a 50mm joist. |

Figures 17 and 18 further illustrate the problems with 50 mm joists. In Figure 17 we see that the screw alignment is hopeless. Few will take the trouble to straighten the joists. The Figure 18 shows the eventual failure of split joists.

Fig. 19. 100x50 joist split face to face.

Not only can 50 mm wide joists split down their full length, when it is only 100 mm high, I have seen them split from face to face as well. I once had our Deckwood specified on a boardwalk but the engineer had ignored our *Deckwood Design Guide* and *Boardwalk Engineering Guide* and specified 100x50 mm KD F11 hardwood. This changed specification is very wrong.[4] I went to the architect with all these pictures and information from the standards and our guides and asked for the design to be changed to a higher grade joist at least 75 mm wide. This was, after all, in line with the much vaunted "manufacturer's instructions". While this was going on, a competitor who simply copied my products without developing a real understanding of them came on the scene and said, "Problem? What problem"? He then took the order without modification to the subframe and also provided a lower specification decking. The deck was then nominated for a design award! Agreed it did photograph well from a distance, but that was all.

At times, I really wonder what hope there is for the timber industry when ignorance of the product sold and a "take the order at all costs" attitude prevails. It is no wonder that there is a buyer resistance to timber.

---

[4] Refer to my guide *Understanding AS2082*

Fig. 20. Staggered screws on a 50mm joist.

Designers persist in specifying 50 mm joists and builders keep trying to make them work. In the example in Figure 20, the builder has understood the need to stagger the screwline and has done so while still using a 50 mm joist. But this arrangement cannot be made to approach anything like the edge clearance requirements of the codes. It is primary school mathematics. The shank diameter of a 14# batten screw measures 6.3 mm. We have found that the screw must be in at least 4 diameters from the edge i.e. 24 mm. This means that you can only stagger 2 mm on a 50 mm joist but you need to stagger at least 16mm (more if you can) meaning that a 75 mm joist is the smallest that can be used with a 14# screw.

But going to a 75 mm joist does not solve all problems. It must be a 75 mm joist in conjunction with best building practice. Figure 21 shows a 75 mm joist but the builder has gone overboard with the screws, three per board and in a straight line. The joist has split despite being wider. The first time I showed this image in a PowerPoint on joist design, a local government engineer in the room laughed. I replied, "Don't laugh. This is in your shire and you will pay to fix it." Bad building practice is no laughing matter. It is all the more tragic when you consider that every pack of this Deckwood decking had installation instructions stapled to it and were ignored! I live in hope that one day someone will actually read the instructions provided.

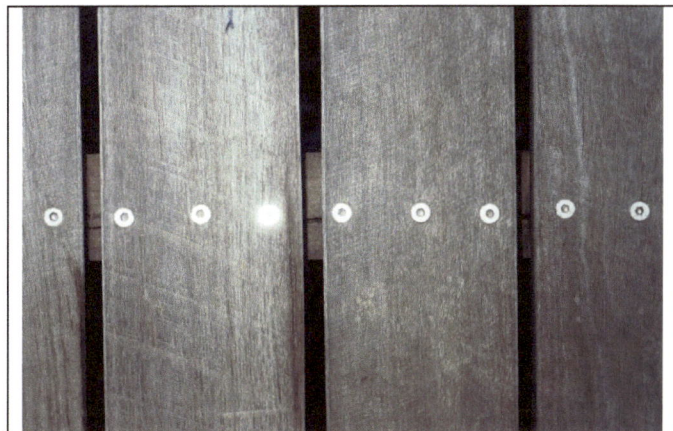

Fig. 21. Split 75mm joist.

Fig. 22. Correctly installed screws. Image courtesy of James Pierce and Associates

Dampcourses

The boardwalk where Figure 22 was taken went through two 1 in 100 year floods floods at about 5 m/s in as many months. A set of piles was washed out so the boardwalk needed repairs to a couple of panels. The boardwalk was built by a "work for the dole" crew of unskilled teenagers but with our *Boardwalk Construction Guide* in one hand. They staggered the screw line and fully predrilled. A layer of CN emulsion would have been applied to the top surface at construction. The top surface of the deck was in excellent order.

Fig. 23. Malthoid with CN Emulsion. Note use of a metal gauge to space decking

We had noticed that while pre-drilling and staggering generally was satisfactory on most joists, some still showed minor splitting. We then adopted a "belts and braces" approach which was to stagger and pre-drill but also to add a layer of Malthoid dampcourse. The CN emulsion was then added to the top of the dampcourse. It has been suggested that CN emulsion should be added to the top of the joist also. The issue of whether to use dampcourses and how to use them is discussed further on under the topic *Malthoid, A Mixed Blessing*.

When using CN emulsion on sawn edges with or without dampcourses it is important that the manufacturer's instructions **not** be followed. The 6 mm coating that is specified works well on end grain but not on sawn edges of hardwood. It will squeeze out under the decking and contaminate the site. Just use a good heavy coating on the top of (and under?) the Malthoid, say 1 mm to a maximum of 2 mm thickness.

Using Triple/Multigrips

Fig. 24. Broken stainless triple grips.

Fig. 25. Failed galvanised triple grips.

My friends at Pryda (and others of course) manufacture triple grips and multigrips from lightly galvanised sheets which are quality items. They also manufacture the same products from stainless steel which are high quality products. Our recommendation about not using triplegrips in boardwalks and decks is not about quality, but about appropriateness.

The two images I have used show triple/multigrips that have failed. The stainless grip in Figure 24 failed due to wave action and the boardwalk that came off its headstock in Figure 25 was due to a flood. Triple/multigrips are excellent at resisting uplift. They are not good at resisting irregular forces.

Even if the boardwalk is well above any predicted flood event, triple grips should not be used as:

- Invariably the "stainless" designation will be left off the specification
- It is very difficult to straighten heavy joists when attached to the headstocks with grips. This is necessary to avoid the poor screw alignment seen in Figure 17.

In the early days, we built a boardwalk designed by a firm of engineers who almost followed our Boardwalk Design Guide to the letter but they had substituted stainless multigrips for bolts. We did not know the consequence then but the builder complained bitterly that the boardwalk was virtually impossible to build. The decking was predrilled and the 150x75 mm joists were all but impossible to straighten when only attached with multigrips but they had to be straightened. Some years afterwards, the same firm designed another boardwalk and cut and pasted the original drawing, as you do, and specified our Deckwood. We notified the engineer of the problems we experienced in the earlier construction but they declined to change their detail. So, having done my part, and as my company wasn't actually building it, I accepted the order for $3000 worth of stainless multigrips. On the first day the builder started placing joists he rang me saying "Will you take the multigrips back. I can't straighten the joists. We are going to bolt them now."

"Sorry, they were a special order."

Bolted connections

Fig. 26. Even bolted joists are not straightforward.

A simple bolted joint is far preferable to using triple grips but even this is not straightforward. Our *Boardwalk Design Guide* gives sizes that are achievable and sustainable under the Queensland forest agreements. Generally we would use a 150 mm joist with a 150 mm bearer giving a total thickness of 300 mm and at most a 350 mm depth. The image shows a 300 mm bearer with a 200 mm joist, i.e. 500 mm. Auger bits do not drill in a straight line even if you have started off square (and that is enough of a challenge). The auger tends to follow the grain and has a mind of its own where it comes out, regardless of how square the bit was when first started. We have found some designers pick span/600 for the deflection limit which is too small and can only be achieved with very large member sizes, so problems like this arise. As there are no plaster joints to pop, greater deflection can be allowed and, after all, the theoretical load of 5 kPa used in our Guides is not achievable anyway. Refer to the Boardwalk Design Guide for deflection limits allowed by Outdoor Structures. These deflections are more realistic and result in achievable sizes and practicality in construction.

Bolt and Screw Type

The issue of corrosion of fasteners in treated timber and different environments is discussed in my *Timber Preservation Guide* so it is not repeated here. To summarise a long detailed and well referenced argument, do not specify galvanised bolts but instead use 304 or 316 grade stainless steel bolts or threaded rod[5]. The corrosion resistance of 304 and 316 stainless steel is very similar and who really cares if the bolts tea stain. No one sees them. We would only go the extra expense of 316 stainless when it is used above the deck in hardware such as wire rope.

Some years ago we had received written advice from one manufacturer that they would not certify their 316 stainless steel screws when used with hardwood joists. On the basis of this we advised clients that they **needed** to use 304 stainless screws. Since then I have received new advice saying,

> "Regarding the use of 316 screws with hardwood decking, it's a great combination, in fact Austenitic stainless (304 or 316) is the best screw material to use in combination with hardwood or softwood decking. 316 (and 304) stainless steel screws are a lot softer than carbon steel screws, and so they can flex a great deal without breaking as the timber changes in moisture content.

---

[5] The use of threaded rod is explained in our *Boardwalk Construction Guide*. It also is not straightforward.

The only issue of stainless screws and hardwood decking timber that I can think of would be that for some screws you may need to countersink the hole as the screw may not be strong enough to pull the head below the surface."[6]

Our recommendation now is that you **should** use 304 stainless as, apart from the unnecessary price difference, it is desirable for the screws to tea stain quickly and so become less obvious. The 304 screws will outlast the decking.

Getting the Lengthwise Joist layout Right

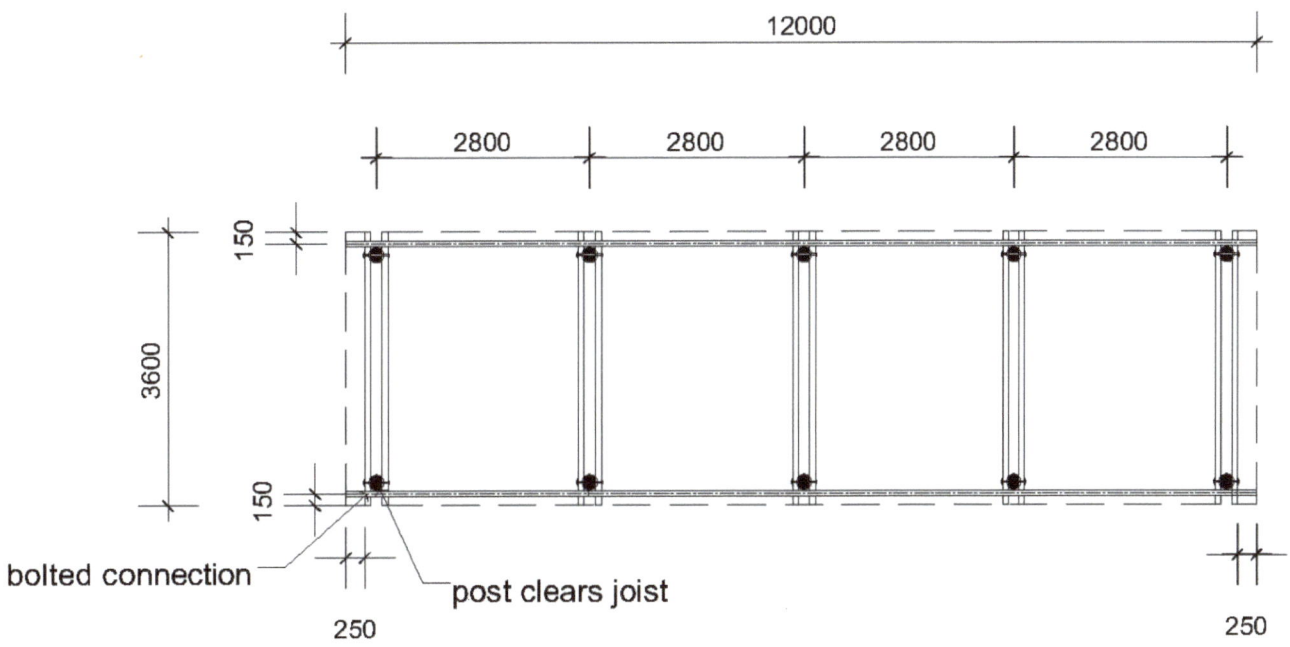

Fig. 27. Draw in outer joists.

So, by now, hopefully, we can see the value of a 75 mm joist with a simple bolted connection. I have drawn in the outer joists and to keep the bolt end clearances on the headstock and on the decking. The centre of the bearer is 250 mm from the end of the deck and the joist is 150 mm from the edges. Unfortunately, we cannot quite make the desired end clearance, after allowing for the 50 mm weathering, where the joists abut on the headstock so extra detailing is required.

Another reason for the 150 mm offset of the joist from the end of the headstock is that it is an appropriate distance for the unrestrained end of decking. Our observation is that this overhang should only extend to 200 mm if the ends are hidden under a kerb. (See Figure 107 where the significance of movement in unrestrained ends is shown).[7] The screws are also well back from the end so no splitting occurs. Obviously, this end clearance cannot happen with a joist right on or very close to the edge.

---

[6] David Collinson, Technical and Product Development Manager, ITW Buildex. *Pers. Com.* June 18, 2012.
[7] The decking with the unrestrained ends shown in Figure 107 is pine so the movement is much more than would be expected with royal species hardwood.

The butted external joists are one of the problem areas of the design and need extra detailing. This is not so with the central joists which are well protected from the weather. Moisture can enter between the two ends of the joists and be held by capillary action and eventually cause decay. We would recommend cutting the outer joists at a small angle so they touch at the top and have a small gap at the bottom of say 10 mm. Combine this with a liberal coating of CN emulsion and there should not be any trouble.

Fig. 28. Gap at bottom of outer joists and headstock bolt arrangement

The importance of this detail only becomes important when we understand the time spans we are talking about. The *Timberlife* prediction software estimates the life of the inner joists when correctly detailed and situated in South East Queensland at 85 years. Your mindset should be, "How do I get this subframe to go to 85 years?" not 15 or 20 or even 30 years.

Figure 28 shows a single headstock bolt. This is preferable as shrinkage is then not an issue. Wherever possible, the headstock should not be checked into the post to avoid trapping moisture. Where checking the post to create a seat for the headstock cannot be avoided, ensure that a liberal coat of CN emulsion to the checkout is specified (and applied).

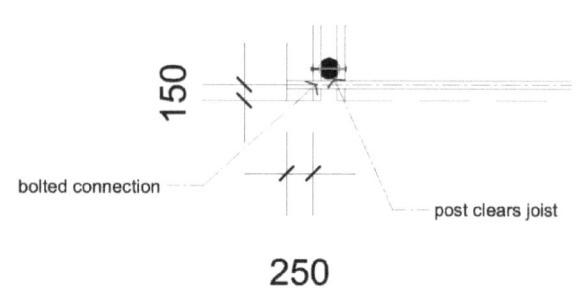

Fig. 29. Joist position in relation to post.

The position of the joist impacts upon the post/pile position. There must be good clearance between the post and the joist. A reasonable allowance is 50 to 75 mm which allows for a piling tolerance. If there is a clash, the builder will simply take to the post with a chainsaw to make the joist fit and so the bolt end clearance will be lost.

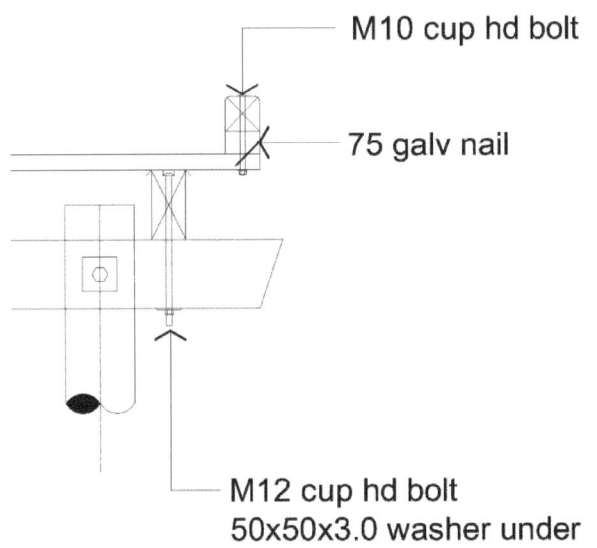

The post/pile needs to be cut shorter than the height of the joist. The pile will not shrink in length but the joist will shrink in height, so clearance is necessary. Generally, 25 mm is all that is needed. If correctly specified, your joists should not shrink more than 6%. This is taken care of if you receive Outdoor Structures Joistwood. Don't forget to use CN emulsion on the top of pine and hardwood posts and the addition of Pryda PoleCats[8] on the top of hardwood posts.

Fig. 30. Clearance under post.

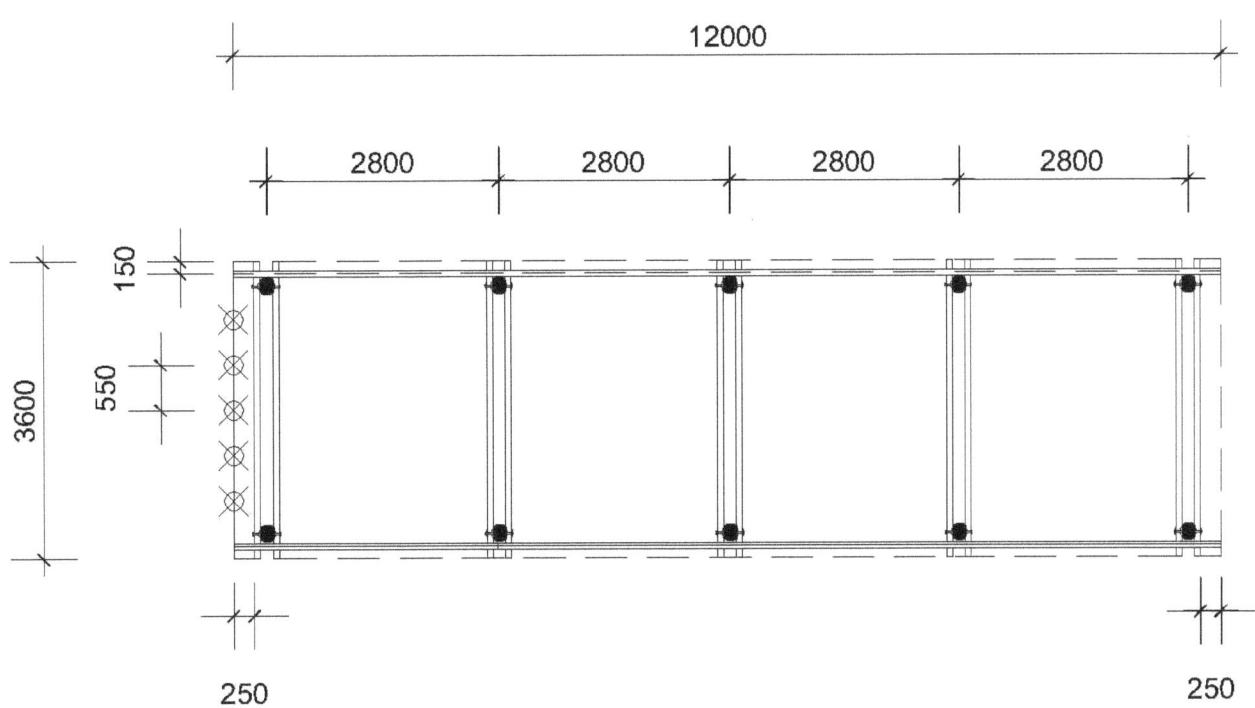

Fig. 31. Determining position of lapped joists.

Determine the positions of the joists which, in this example, will be at 550 mm. Note that this is not the centreline of the joists as such but the line on which the staggered joists are aligned. Staggering the joists means that one of the spacings is actually 75 mm larger. So, when working out the spacing, we do

---

[8] Another invention from the people who set up OSA.

not work to the maximum spacing of the decking but keep back about 75 mm.

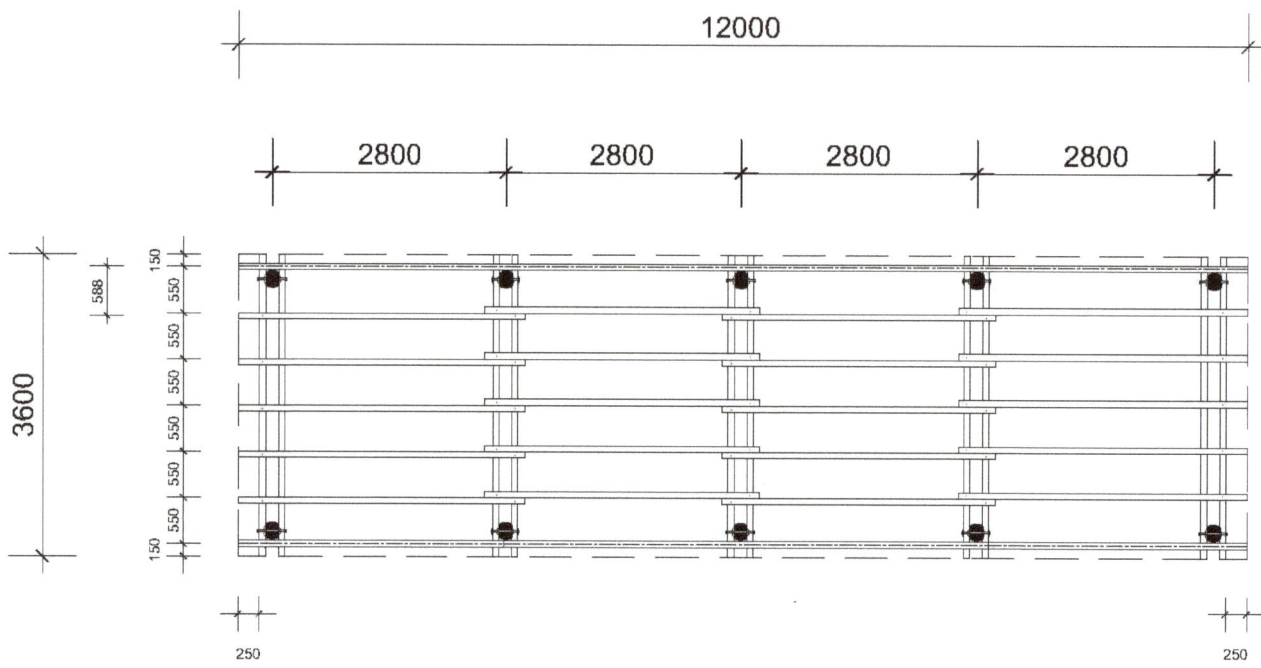

Fig. 32. Lapped joists in place

The next step is to draw in the staggered joists. There are many reasons for adopting this alignment over the conventional arrangement. The less important reasons, which still justify utilising this method of construction, are:

- Less cutting and sawdust on site for environmentally sensitive areas – (decking and headstocks can be supplied pre-cut and the decking pre-drilled)
- Lower skill level needed
- No need to remove sawdust or offcuts
- Structure is tied together better as:
  o The joists are bolted on the furtherest headstock
  o Two bolts can be fitted to each joist end if needed.

Fig. 33. Example of lapped joists.

The most important reason, however, is safety. With the normal aligned arrangement, the screws go right up to the end of the joist and no amount of best practice by staggering the screwline will stop the end of the joist splitting. Once the end has split, the screws simply have little holding power, allowing the deck to cup/move and potentially result in a trip hazard. Of course, lapping the joists means that the screw line is not straight. This can catch the eye, especially when the screws are new and shiny. One architect was adamant that he did not want this effect and that the screws must be staggered over a single straight line but was conscious of the need to still provide a safe deck. An alternative we provided were Pryda stainless steel nail plates for the end of the joists. I cannot check if it has worked. It should have.

Fig. 34. Decking lifting due to split joist ends.

Note: It is common to see a similar effect to what is shown in Figure 34 when heavy pine decking is screwed to 50mm pine joists with 10# screws.

It is not satisfactory to do nothing. We used to supply a lot of timber to Japan. There, the architects would point blank refuse even to stagger the screwline because even that was an affront to the senses, or at least to theirs. Royal species hardwood is a wonderful product and has the potential (it doesn't happen automatically) to build decks and boardwalks of exceptional durability. Despite timber's many strengths, it also has some weaknesses and hand in hand with utilising its strength and beauty is the need to accommodate its weakness. If a designer is not prepared to do this he/she needs to look for a different medium for the subframe but then find they are dealing with a completely unexpected set of difficulties. Refer to the section *Decking on Steel Joists*.

Running the Decking Lengthways

The joist layout for crosswise decking is much simpler than for decking running lengthwise. A lot more thought has to be given to the joist positions. We start with the same deck measuring 12x3.6 m.

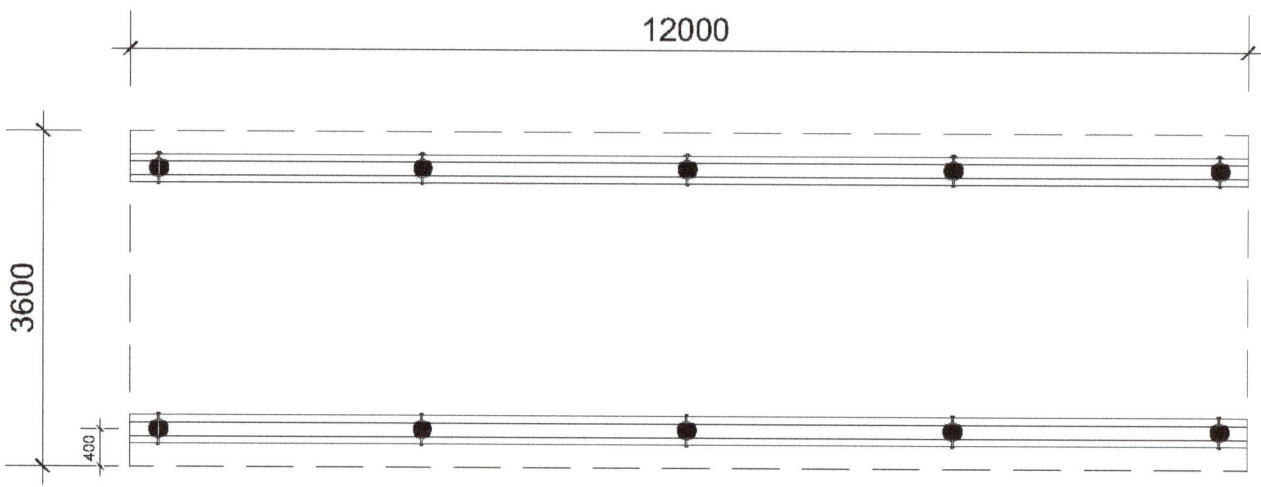

Fig. 35. Determine position of headstocks.

The first stage is to draw in the double headstocks, again keeping the end clearances as with the crosswise deck. I have set the piles/posts at equal centres. We will return to this decision later in the Guide.

Fig. 36. Example of a spliced bearer.

Obviously, timber 12 m long is not available so it will have to be joined. If you join on the posts the end clearances cannot be maintained. Our practice was to establish a structural connection at the pile/post and then splice the next bearer to the well connected one. There are other ways of doing this such as with metal plates, but either way it has to be detailed. Do not leave this to the imagination of the builder. Liberally coat the contact faces of the splice with CN Emulsion.

Hopefully, by now I have convinced the designer not to use 50 mm joists but usual practice from here is to again set out the deck like a verandah with 450 to 600 mm spacings and use lineal decking.

Why we Use Set length Decking

Fig. 37. Screws too close to the end.

Fig. 38. Trying to join on a 50mm joist.

When lineal decking is used, you have 75 mm on which to rest the two pieces of decking and insert four screws. It is not enough, yet some try to do it on 50 mm. 75 to 100 mm of end clearance is needed to ensure there is no end splitting of the decking. To achieve this we must use set length material, not lineal.

The aim of the layout I will demonstrate will be to plan the location of the joins and maintain the screw end clearance. It is probably wise to specify that the joists are to be sized to 3 to 5 mm under the nominated size. The double joists have to be matched in size and all the builder has to do is to measure them and pick his double joists but in practice it is all too much trouble for most builders.

Fig. 39. Decking join over double joist.

Fig. 40. Decay in the end of decking.

Designing to a Module

The arrangement we are aiming for with set lengths also allows us to build in a 5 to 6 mm gap between the ends of the boards. A problem often seen on decks is decay at the end of the boards where they are butted up tight. Moisture enters the end grain and decay eventually has to occur. The detailing that follows completely avoids this.

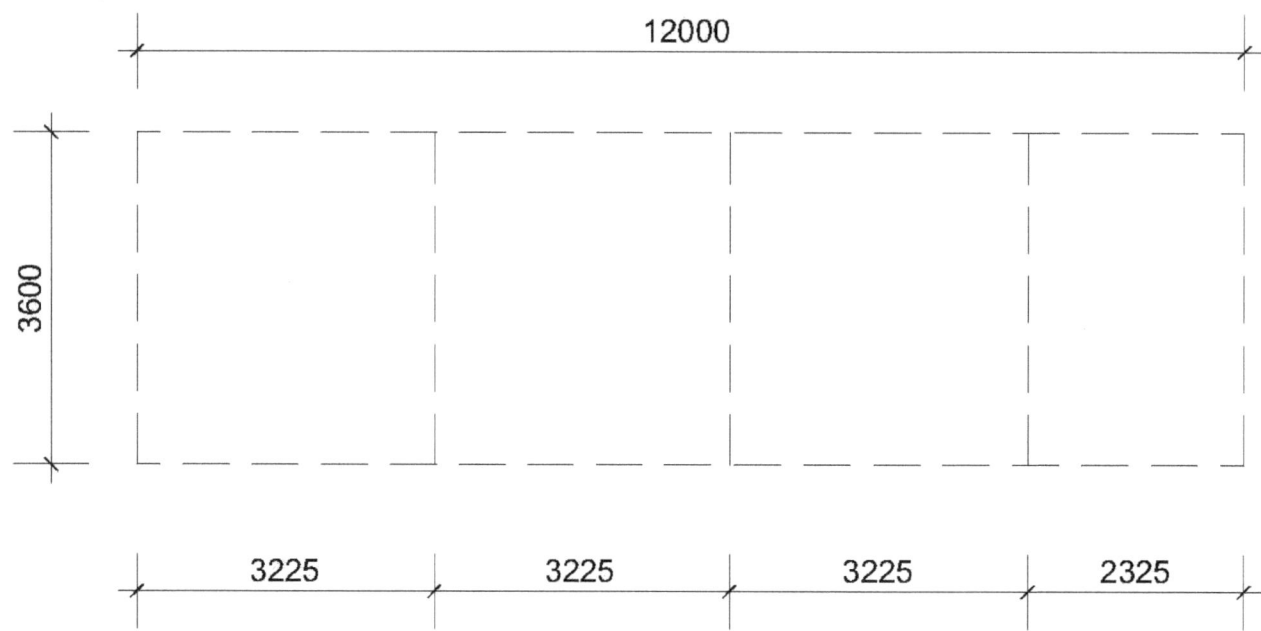

Fig. 41. Determining module for decking.

A good module to use on our 12 m deck would be three boards at 3.3 m and one at 2.4 m. These are easy lengths for the miller and give good recovery from the saw logs. Supply should be quicker and the price minimised.

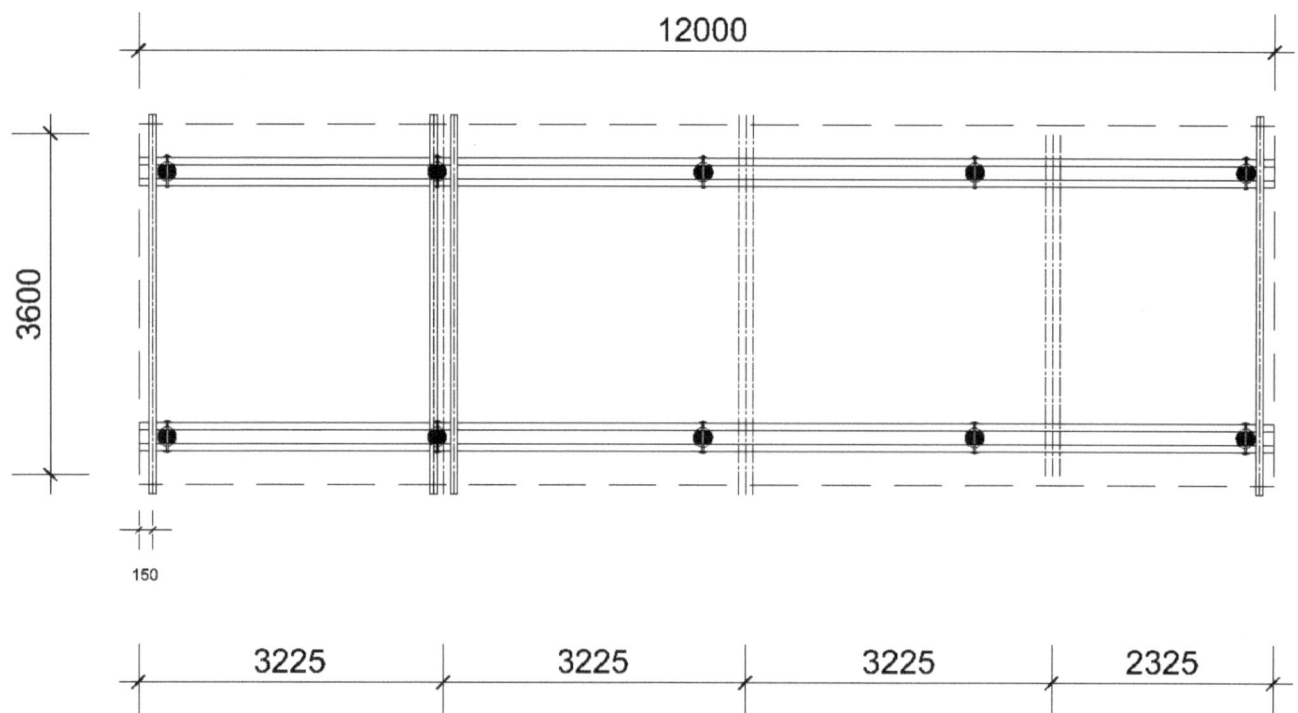

Fig. 42. Draw in the joists which have fixed positions.

The end joists maintain the same end clearance as with the cross deck and the first joists are positioned. The double joists are centred over the module with the inner face of the paired joist 75 mm either side of the module, i.e. 150 mm apart. The joists extend past the outside line of the deck by a minimum of 100 mm. This helps prevent the end of the joists from splitting and so allowing the screws in the edge boards from working out. If the joists must be finished level with the outside of the deck, consider using stainless nailplates to hold the ends together. By the time the nail plate is forced out the joist end should be stable. Put a weathering (sloping) cut on the joists. Ensure dampcourse is extended over the end of the joist and around the weathering cut.

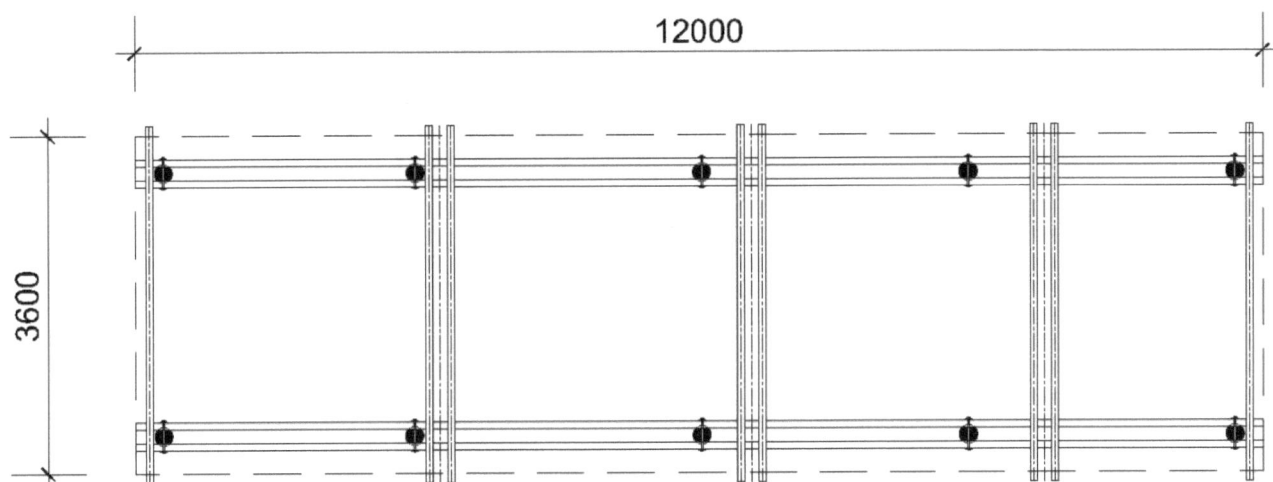

Fig. 43. Move posts that clash with joists.

You would have noticed that one set of piles/posts has clashed with one set of double joists. In this case I have simply moved the post so there was no conflict with the joist. Again a piling tolerance needs to be maintained.

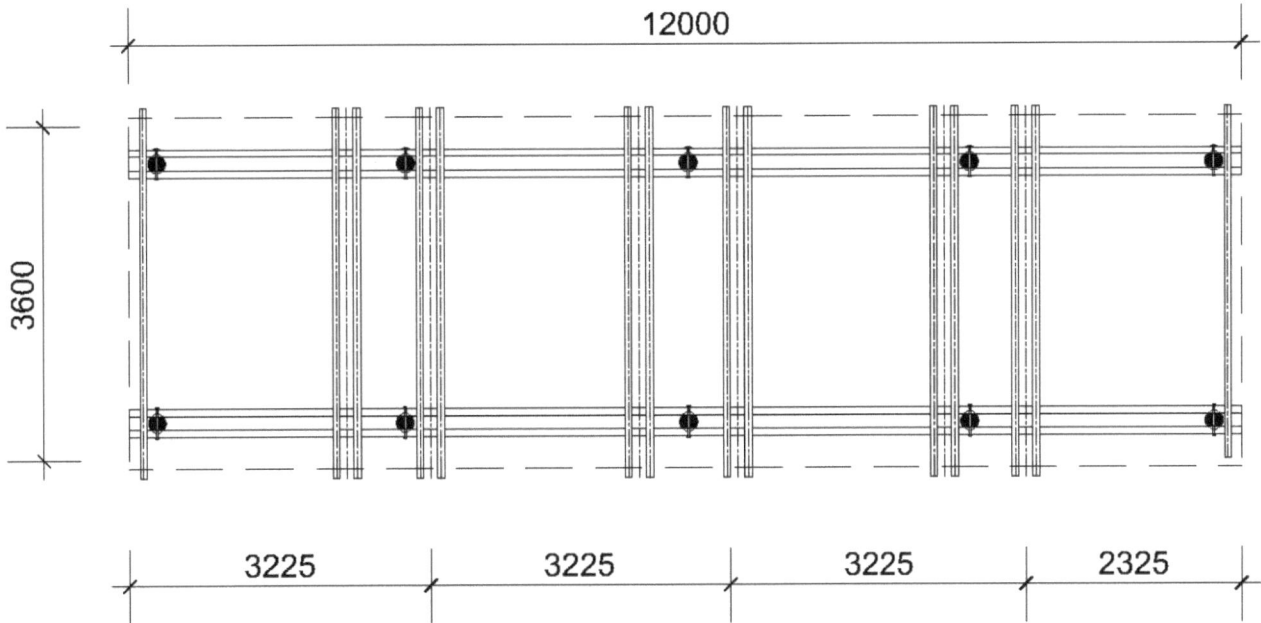

Fig. 44. Mirror positions of double joists.

The next stage is to mirror the double joists. Again I have moved the second set of posts so they no longer clash rather than adjust the joist position.

Note: When laying out a wider deck that needs three or more bearers, keep the double joists in a straight line like the outer joists in Figure 27. You can lap them but it gets a bit complicated for the builder and the join pattern doesn't look quite right. Also see comments about nailplates after Figure 35.

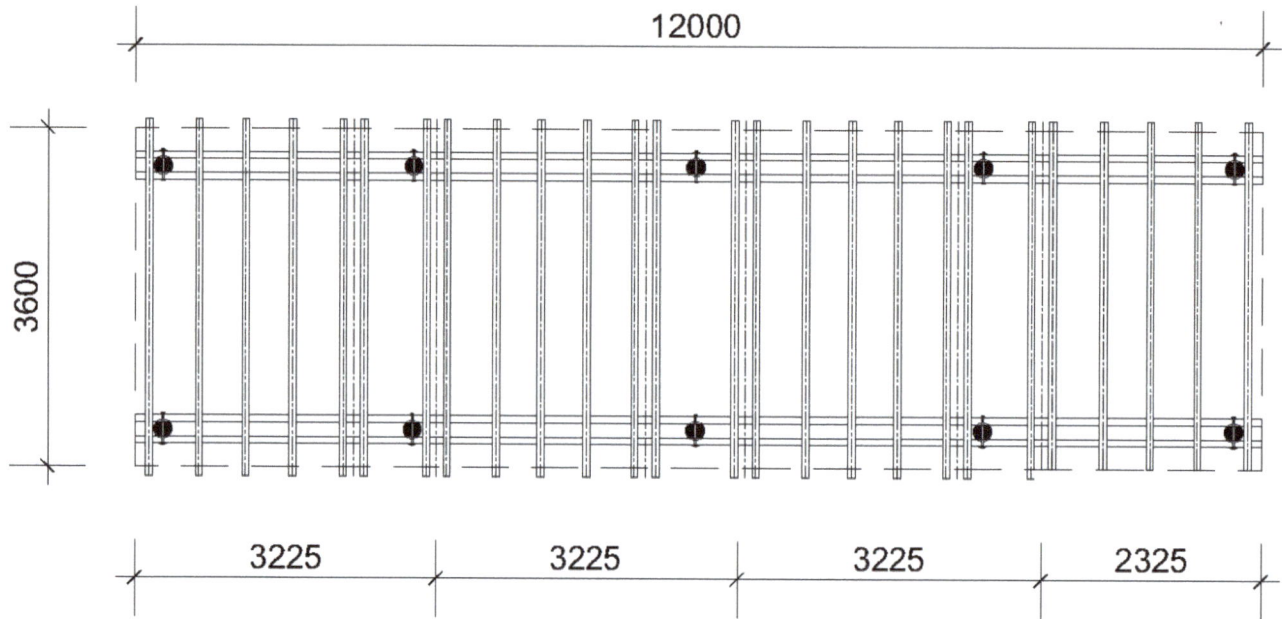

Fig. 45. Draw in position of joists between pairs of double joists.

Fill in each panel between the double joists with joists spaced equal distance within each panel. In practice, the spacing may not be the same from panel to panel.

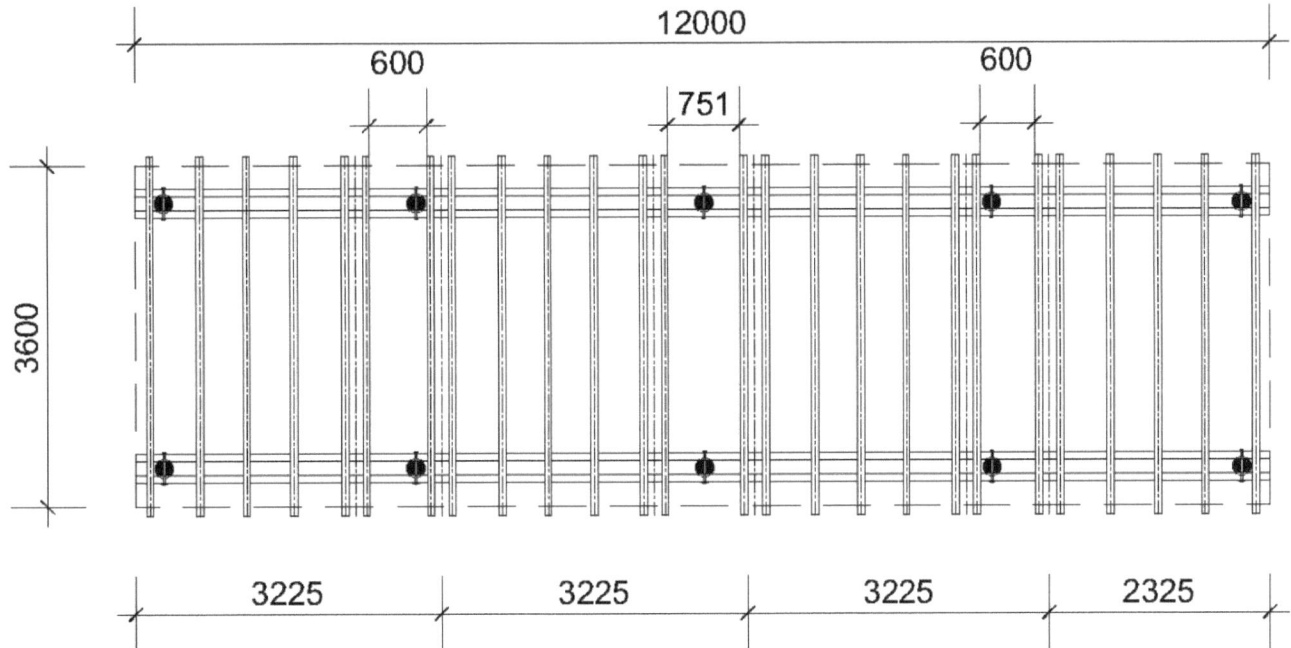

Fig. 46. Check the distance inside the pairs of double joists

Check the decking spans at the double joist pairs. In this case, there are two at 600 mm which is within the span allowance of the decking and one at 751 mm. The larger measurement is too far to span the decking so a joist needs to be added.

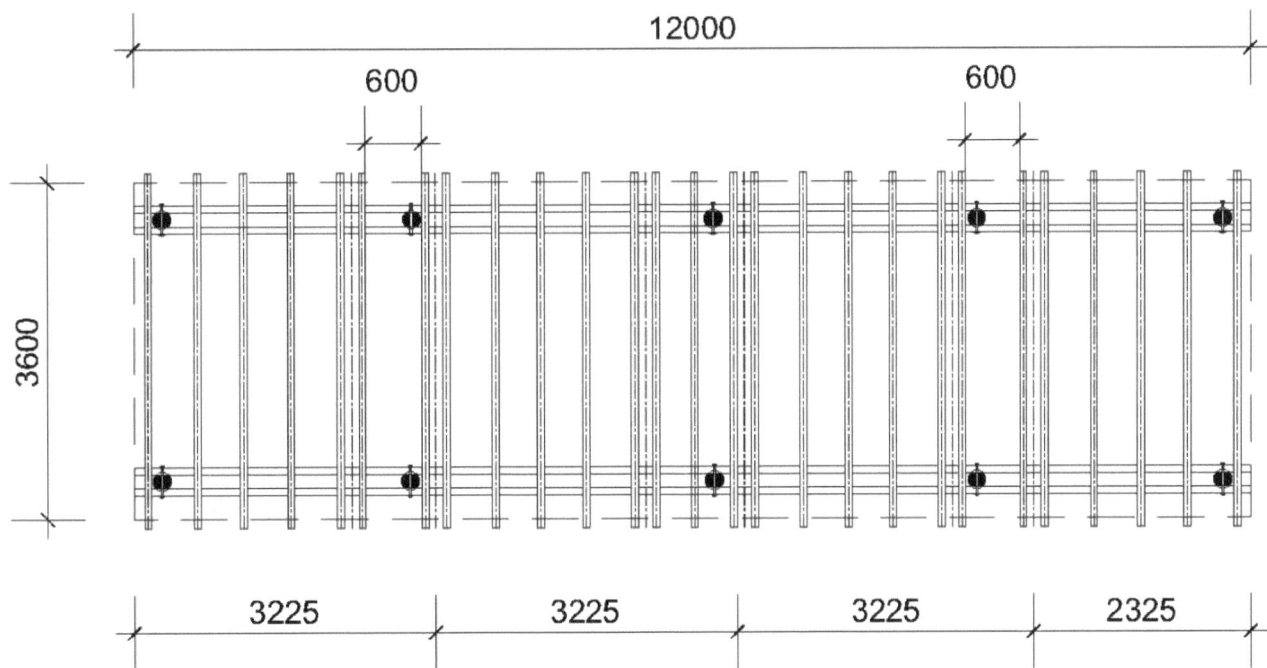

Fig. 47. Draw in remaining joists as needed.

The final joist is drawn but again it clashes with a pile/post. Yet again I have moved the pile/post to avoid a clash.

The spacing between the joists where decking is running lengthways is not likely to be uniform but it is not especially complex to lay out. The drawings showing the joist positions should be fully dimensioned and nothing left to the builder's imagination. It is invariably "too much trouble"[9] for the builder to work this out and some do not have the ability as it is so different from what they would normally do.

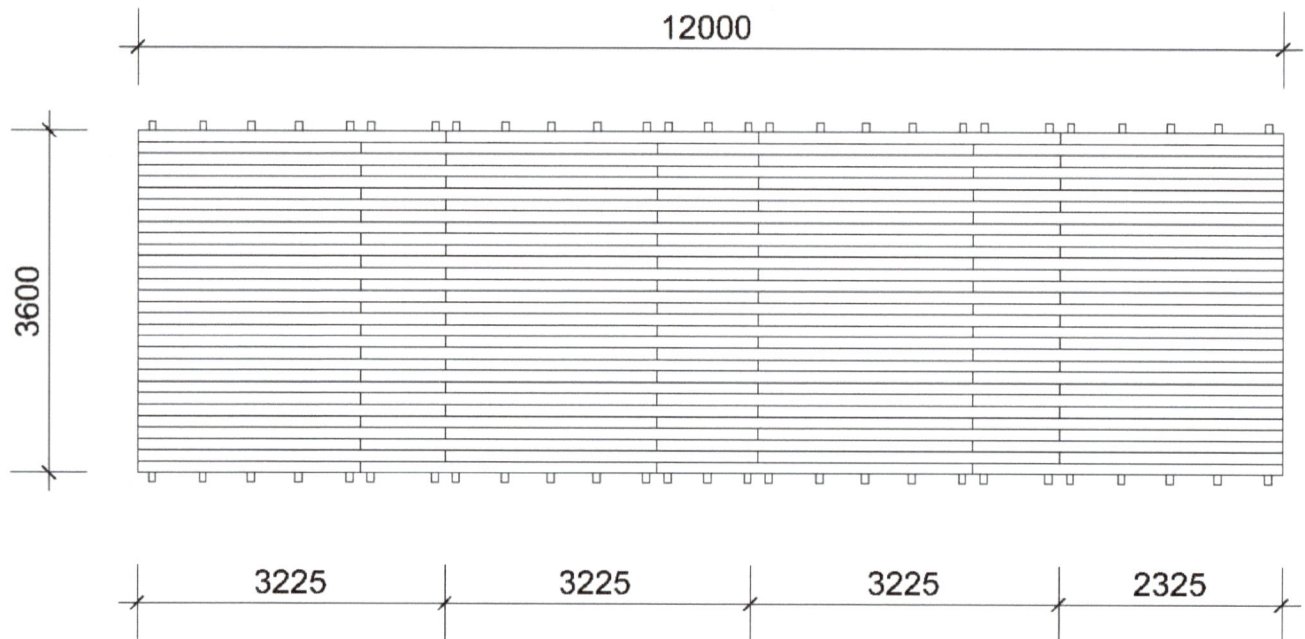

Fig. 48. Final layout of decking.

The final deck has joins that are intentional and planned. There isn't a straight line where the boards join which adds extra strength. The end result looks right.

Foundation issues

Pier, Joist and Handrail Interaction

When detailing the deck running lengthways, there were three pile/post clashes so I simply moved them as that is very easy to do in CAD. But was I right to do so or should I have moved the joists? It all depends, consider these three examples.

---

[9] We designed and supplied a deck at a hotel for the same builders with badly split joists in Figure 13. Our deck combined all the features we described under Deck Design 101. I was told by one of their employees "It was too much trouble". Trouble, yes. Too much? Far from it.

Fig. 49. Boardwalk without handrail.

At first glance we would say that, with the boardwalk in Figure 49, it does not matter whether you design for the joist or post position as there is no handrail to consider. But as this deck is built on very expensive double treated marine piles driven from a barge, the main consideration here should be to minimise the number of piles so their placement is critical. So we would say the pile positions should govern.

The handrail posts on the deck in Figure 50 are fitted in-between the double headstocks so regular spacings on the posts were necessary to give equal handrail modules. Again, post position governs the layout.

Fig. 50. Deck with equal spaced handrail.

Fig. 51. Steel posts on timber deck.

Fig. 52. Steel posts attachment detail.

The posts supporting the deck in Figure 51 are spaced further apart than the handrail posts so there is no attempt to sit one above another. The standard steel handrail post support of Outdoor Structures (Figure 52) is designed to bolt straight to the deck or straddle the joist if there is a clash. Joist positioning would be more important here to maintain equal spacing on the handrail posts.

These examples show that there is not one answer to the question of whether post or joist position governs design.

Perhaps some designers may think that the system I am outlining might cramp their creativity. It is a bit like cars. They all look much the same these days. It is not surprising as there is, at the end of the day, one most efficient shape. Likewise with timber, there is only best practice up to deck level. Where professional designers have an edge is that the aesthetics is all in the handrail and so they can stamp their creativity on a standard deck. While handrail design is not covered in the scope of this Guide[10] we have observed that it can almost be an afterthought, I have a deck, now how do I fit a handrail? However, handrail must be considered from the earliest stages of the design, and arguably may be even the first part of the design due to its integration with both joists and piles/posts.

Pile/Post Design

Foundation design is not part of this guide as soil and water conditions vary too much to even attempt it. This design needs to be undertaken by a professional engineer, and ideally one familiar with timber. Our various guides do offer assistance however. While I believe royal species hardwood of appropriate grades and profiles is the best material from which to build the superstructure of boardwalks and decks, in most applications it is hard to go past a H5 treated pine post for economy, ease of handling and longevity.

There are four things to consider in your foundation design relating to durability that can be overlooked:

- The effectiveness of treatment in some products. (It means very little on sawn timber!)
- Decay at groundline (particularly when embedded in concrete).
- The effect of notches through a treatment envelope
- The effect of fire.

Guidance on these matters is given in the relevant sections of my *Timber Preservation Guide*.

Standard boardwalk foundation pile/bearer configurations are given in the *Boardwalk Design Guide*. The pile/post sizes nominated are generally sufficient for heights Above-Ground of 1.5m. Where local conditions are more taxing than normal, e.g. constantly moist, it is easy to go up from say a 150 mm diameter post to 200 mm as the material cost is relatively inexpensive.

When soil tests have to be conducted for major decks on piled foundations, advice on the geotechnical investigation is given in the *Light Bridge Manual*.

In about 2004 I had been promised a good size boardwalk order. The designer had followed our guides for the superstructure fairly closely but not when it came to the posts. They were just F17 hardwood. We drew to our potential customer's attention that they could expect early failure as the timber did not have sufficient durability. With the addition of embedding in concrete, all design certainty was lost. Next thing I knew the order went to a small bush mill. In those days I retained a naive hope that the client would have listened and would have changed the foundation design. I visited the boardwalk and saw that the foundation was unchanged and the spotted gum posts (In-Ground Durability Class 2) were simply set in concrete. I later spoke to the miller who provided the timber saying, "What were you thinking of supplying those posts? You know they are wrong."

---

[10] Refer to our *Commercial Barrier Guide*.

"I know," was the response. "But I had to or I would not have got the order." This was at the start of 10 years of drought which meant almost "anything goes" at groundline. The designer probably thinks I don't know the basics of timber design but doesn't realise he/she was just lucky. Design certainty is not about luck, it is about intent.

The lesson is that suppliers will fall over themselves in the rush to supply whatever you ask for as your foundations. Be sure you are asking for the right thing. Many of the landscaping projects will be subject to irrigation and fertiliser. This accelerates ground line decay.

Fig. 53. Spotted gum post set in concrete.

Decking Issues

Ideal Decking Lengths

Consider the decking shown in Figure 17. It is long, at least 6 m. What you do not see in the image is that the timber is also of a lower grade than Deckwood. Consider then the tree that the decking will be cut from. It may have been growing for 60 years. During its long life it has been subject to droughts, floods, insect attacks and throw in the occasional termite and a myriad of other things that impact on timber quality. On top of this the tree is round(ish), tapered and seldom especially straight. Yet, as illogical as it seems, there is still the misconception that such logs will cut large volumes of long, high quality timber! Of course you can still get this as house framing but decking is not house framing and claims of meeting an inappropriate framing grade is no guarantee of quality or suitability for decking. House frames do not see the weather or a critical eye.

Fig. 54. The consequence of attempting to supply to an F grade.

Decking needs a virtually clear face to weather well. You do not get this with F rated timber. Frequently people will ask for F14 hardwood and that is all they ask for. Sometimes designers will buck the trend and ask for the more expensive F17 thinking that this will beat the failures by others. Ironbark graded to F17 can have an unsound knot covering 1/3 of the face, have unlimited tight gum vein and 20% of its cross section missing. You may as well write the decking specification as "just give it a cursory glance and if it is really, really bad I would prefer you do not put it in"[11]. For years the parties involved have been specifying, allowing, producing and/or supplying and using such material but it doesn't make it suitable, and it doesn't make it professional. It never was and never will be.

The likelihood of finding natural feature in a piece of decking will increase in direct ratio to its cross section. The harder the piece is to cut, and the lower the likelihood of utilising any falldown, the lower the standard of what is permitted in the order will be. This is the problem with long decking. The deck in Figure 17 would have been far higher quality if it was supplied as a 3.6 m and a 2.4 m and laid with staggered joins. In the milling process the miller would have cut billets from his logs at 3.6 m, which allows him to cut at the bends in the logs. This leaves his straight logs for structural members that need long lengths. By cutting the log he also maximises the recovery as it deals better with its taper. As he cuts the 3.6 m logs some of the decking will have too much defect. When it comes to the grading and defect docking part of production, most of these out of grade pieces would have been docked to 2.4m. This is clever and environmentally responsible use of the resource.

When we produced Deckwood we would purchase a trailer load of timber of the nominated species and graded <u>allegedly</u> to have one good face. Then the packs would be run through the planer, re-graded to a uniform quality and defect docked (mill grading often left much to be desired) and then sorted into lengths prior to treatment. There were very few long lengths as a proportion to the whole. Our experience drawn from years as millers and decking specialists is that you should discipline yourself to work to 3.6 m, perhaps stretching it out to 4.2 m and longer lengths not exceeding 10% of the total.

Australian readers are fortunate to have available to them some of the world's very best hardwoods. Throughout this guide it is assumed that these hardwoods will be used as decking. Unfortunately, through poor specification of the durable species, quality or installation practices some hardwood decks have not performed well. To solve this some have used different decking materials, not realising that they are adopting a very different and often poorly understood set of problems. To assist designers considering using alternatives we have included an analysis of different decking materials written by the

---

[11] AS2082 will still allow the producer to supply 5% of the total with the really, really bad material in!

prominent Brisbane Architect, Ralph Bailey of Guymer Bailey Architects. This is found in Appendix B

Recycled or New Timber?

I believe that the Interim standards for decorative and for recycled timber are unsuitable for boardwalk decking! This is explained in detail in our guide, *Understanding AS2082*. To function well, decking needs to be extremely high durability and virtually clear of natural feature whereas recycled timber was originally conceived around "character pieces".

I showed the picture of the decking with a large defect in Figure 55 to an "authority" in the timber industry fresh from England and asked how long would it last. He could see no problem. He grabbed

Fig. 55. Recycled Decking

AS5604 Timber Natural durability ratings and looked up Table 1 and said "40 years". His superior came in at that point and looked at the same picture and said "4 to 5 years". That would be my expectation. It is not good enough for a product that is much more expensive to purchase than new timber (about 20-25 year life expected). I expect that the deck in Figure 55 cost the client hundreds of thousands of dollars extra for this quality of timber either for green points or warm fuzzy feelings. No amount of green points or the "warm and fuzzies" can compensate a child in hospital who has badly gashed open his/her foot and that is what this quality timber does.

By all means ask for recycled decking but do not drop the quality below what would be appropriate in new timber (Structural Grade 1 for the face, not an F rating) or species requirements. Your challenge will be to find someone who can supply it from tired worn out timber. Do not accept grading to the recycled standards. As well, do not expect it to be seasoned even if it is 100 years old as, in all likelihood it would have been cut from round timber that was too large to dry. Invariably it acts like new timber once re-sawn.

Incidentally, the decking in Figure 55 has what is termed in the trade a "rougher headed" finish in an attempt to emulate a rough sawn finish. Rougher heading is a dressed surface with a very fine reeded finish. I expect that this will deteriorate fairly rapidly compared to a standard natural sawn finish.

Slip Resistance and Surface Finish

Fig. 56. Pendulum slip resistance meter on dressed decking finished with Intergrain film finish.

If I have learnt anything about timber, much of that knowledge has come largely through listening and acting on what I heard. We have been manufacturing a reeded version of Deckwood for gangways from the outset. These were short lengths and people always walked over them against the reed. Initially it seemed a good idea to use them as bridge decks too and, in the early days, I supplied a few bridge decks in it as well. Then I supplied a bridge deck which had a 90 degree bend at an approach ramp. Not long afterwards one of my friends in that council rang me and said "Ted, don't do that again. People are slipping over as they go around the bend." So much for making assumptions! Since that day I reverted to only selling reeded decking in short length decking for gangways where the possible increased grip may offset the shorter life caused by water sitting in the reeds.

To be frank, I do not know much about slip resistance in timber decking, but then nobody else seems to either. I could not find any definitive information through Timber Queensland. We had discussions with people in the Home Modification and Maintenance Clearinghouse Project of the Faculty of Health Sciences at the University of Sydney about this subject following some initial tests I did. We agreed that authoritative answers could only be provided by a PHD student spending years on the subject. Factors that could affect slip resistance are:

- Dressed or rough surface
- Species
- Oiled or not oiled
- Type of oil
- Age of the decking
- Walking with or against the grain.

It is even very uncertain what the best test to use is, the pendulum or sloping ramp test. We tried to raise joint funding for this study and it is a pity that it did not happen. The initial testing I did was simply to go out for a day with a pendulum tester, a technician and senior lecturer from the University of Southern Queensland to get a feel for the situation. This was followed up by some formal ramp and pendulum testing.

We checked dressed spotted gum decking with an Intergrain film finish (Figure 56) and there was no surprise. The testing showed that there was a very high likelihood of slipping when wet. Under cover it was high. We were measuring the film, not the timber. Even without a film finish a wet dressed spotted gum deck has to be almost deadly. In the days before webbing load binding straps we had seen decking and floor boards slip out of packs freshly packed with steel bands when we had to deliver them up steep hills. I cannot stress too highly, in our opinion specifying dressed decking in the weather is irresponsible due to the danger of slipping. We would supply dressed face Deckwood only when it is under a roof. But people continue to do it because it looks pretty - (for a while).

Fig. 57. Slip resistance testing on narrow Deckwood.

We also checked the slip resistance of some of our Deckwood with a natural sawn face. Testing with a pendulum on new boards showed a low likelihood of slipping but the likelihood increased on a well worn deck. When the deck boards are aligned crosswise to the direction of travel the risk was low when dry and increased to high when wet. With narrow 70mm boards the risk was low.

There are two problems with the pendulum testing results:

1. A high likelihood of slipping in certain circumstances does not bear out with experience. I have simply sold too much of this material not to have solicitors tapping me on the shoulder if there was a problem.
2. Under certified testing the pendulum and the ramp test gave very different results. The ramp test showed much better slip resistance on the same material.

The ramp test showed a result of R12 for <u>freshly oiled</u> 136x42 KD spotted gum but for the pendulum it was classed as Y. One reading is good and the other is poor. I expect that one is picking up the cogging effect of the decking gaps but that is just a guess. So it still leaves a PhD project for some eager student. It is well known among producers that dressed decking deteriorates far more quickly than natural sawn face decking. Notwithstanding the safety issue, when a designer specifies a dressed face weather exposed deck he/she is in effect saying to the client, "I am going to give you a deck that falls far short of its potential service life."

In the early days of producing Deckwood, we had it specified for the spiral ramp illustrated in Figure 58. The builder, wanting to maximise his profit, substituted another manufacturer's product. I went to see what was purchased and expected to see poor quality decking but it was every bit as good as mine, except that it had a dressed face instead of the natural sawn face which was specified. As I was aware that people were slipping on the deck. I used it in my presentations to illustrate the difference between a quality product and an appropriate product. At one presentation a young engineer laughed, telling the room about the number of times he came off his bike on that ramp when it was wet. The handrail is low and there is a considerable fall height. You sacrifice grip for beauty or economy at the risk of finding out how good your professional indemnity insurance is.

Fig. 58. Quality decking is not always appropriate decking

Self Cleaning Decks

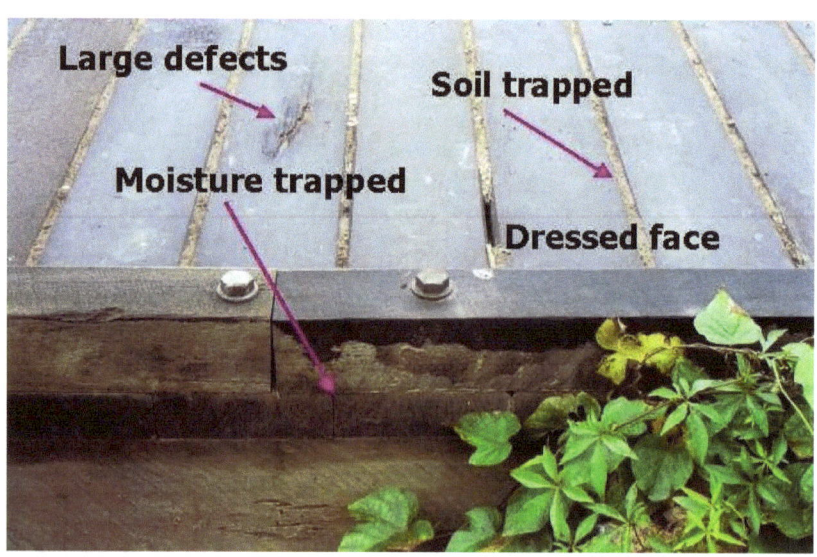

Fig. 59. Decks (and kerbs) need to self clean.

Colin MacKenzie, Technical Director of Timber Queensland, has given three requirements for a long lived timber structure. These are

:
- Keep them dry
- Don't let the rain get to them
- Don't let them get wet!

All three are hard to achieve with boardwalks so the compromise is to detail the structure so it dries as soon as possible. Figure 59 shows a boardwalk that breaks this rule. It shouldn't have, as it was specified in Deckwood but the builder substituted generic decking to save a few dollars.

Figure 59 shows the kerb coach-screwed straight onto the deck. There is no gap between the decking under the kerb but there is a gap once the kerb has been cleared. This means that moisture is trapped between the kerb and the decking which will promote decay. Further, as there is no gap under the kerb, leaf litter is trapped on the deck. A gap of at least 50 mm is needed to clear leaf litter. I once saw a boardwalk in a rainforest decay to the point of being unserviceable because of decay along the kerb to deck interface due to a build-up of leaf litter. There was no gap underneath.

Fig. 60. Underside of parallel sided decking – note moisture.

As well, the decking has parallel sides with an arrised top. The gaps have filled with soil and hold moisture. In our opinion there is not one correct shape for decking. It will depend on width to thickness ratios and depth. But there is one feature in common: they should have tapered sides. My company introduced this shape to Australia and developed the profile until it was able to carry a patent. The advantages of the Deckwood profile are:
- Leaf litter falls through
- Large gap at the joist gives better airflow
- Reeded underside gives better air flow
- Anti warp groove gives stability and airflow

Producers eventually started putting tapered sides on their decking and passing it off as our Deckwood but at a lower price. Of course there was not the species selection or the grading that went into Deckwood but no one seemed to care about substitution with lower grade material unless the customers complained. Appendix B contains a suitable decking specification. A confirmation grading by an independent consultant is recommended.

One thing to notice from Figure 59 is the dangerous natural feature on the top of a dressed surface. Most of the boards in the deck have the rough side up (as they were intended to be) but the builder appears not to have taken the trouble to ensure uniformity in the laying. That board with the defect is laid dressed side up exposing the splinter and so endangers the public. That is why Deckwood is pre-graded and not reversible.

How to Avoid Cupped Decking

Fig. 61. Image of cupped 145x35 decking

While there are references in the Australian Standards to width to thickness ratios for some structural members, there is no such ratio for decking. Deckwood measuring 145x35 mm was a short-lived member of our Deckwood range. After being made aware that it was cupping, this size was withdrawn. Its ratio was 4.1:1, just beyond what is justifiably regarded as "the limit".

Decking of similar ratio cannot be guaranteed to deliver customer satisfaction. Unfortunately, we note that there are still some design offices specifying decking measuring 140x31 mm (ratio 4.5:1). This is even more likely to cup. Our experience is that 120x35 (ratio 3.4:1) and 145x45 mm (ratio 3.2:1) are stable.

Use of unseasoned timber can contribute to cupping due to differential shrinkage between tangential and radial faces but kiln drying decking does not automatically give you stability. Potential to cup is best addressed/minimized by:

- Using 'stocky' cross sections - breadth to depth ratio 3.5:1 max or less
- Use of seasoned timber (try hard to avoid this if possible)[12]
- Application and maintenance with a water repellent finish[13]
- Good ventilation below the deck.

Kiln drying your decking will not eliminate distortion caused by differential moisture between the hot top and cooler back. Kiln drying also introduces delays, greatly increases the carbon footprint of your project and will not counteract an incorrect width to thickness ratio. Timber is no different to steel and concrete in that there are some rules that you break at your peril. By specifying (and receiving) genuine Deckwood we take care of this for you.

---

[12] Refer to *Decking Gaps* where this is expanded upon.
[13] This should be applied all round prior to laying.

Decks and Ground Contact

Designers cannot avoid the simple reality that somehow their structure eventually has to connect with the ground at the end. What you can avoid easily is designing your timber deck so the ground also abuts the edge as it does in Figure 62. Here the joists were buried and the garden spread over the deck and termites were able to work away quite happily unnoticed.

Fig. 62. Garden next to a boardwalk

Fig. 63. Terminating in non durable timber. How not to do it.

When designing your structure, you must do all that is possible to ensure the timber bearers and joists are at least 200mm above the ground. Anything less should be specified as a Durability 1 In-Ground timber. The species in our standard Joistwood perform adequately above that height. If the choice of the durability is left to the lowest tenderer, the assessment will be that this is above ground so I will purchase Durability 1 (if you are lucky) Above-Ground timber.

Ideally, terminate in concrete with sufficient height above ground to maintain the clearance under the joist. We have found a useful detail in connecting with the ground is to have a sacrificial sleeper at the end in a termite resistant, In-Ground Durability 1 timber such as ironbark. We have observed that the conditions around the termination change over time. The way the termination shown in Figure 63 is detailed, soil will migrate around and bury the end turning it into a full blown H5 application.

A frequent problem we have observed is that the deck/boardwalk is built on piles or potted posts and the concrete approach is constructed on fill. The one remains as built. The other settles fairly quickly. A serious trip hazard eventuates. The concrete approach cannot be considered as separate from the deck. With a boardwalk, one way is to continue the posts/piles past the end to support the approach too. The concrete will probably crack but it is better than a broken hip. The particular problem shown in Figure 64 was solved by attaching a section of aluminium checkerplate over the join.

Fig. 64. Differential movement between path and deck.

Another problem I have observed when the deck/boardwalk is at the bottom of a hill is a build-up of soil washed down the slope. The loose material is a slip risk and holds moisture promoting decay. I have seen this dealt with effectively by placing a length of grillage at the approach so any soil falls through.

Shelling Out

The extent of natural feature in a deck can be controlled through careful specification and enforced compliance to that specification. These features can be easily seen, a tape measure placed across them and a clear in/out decision made. Grading requirements only assess timber at the time of milling and if a grader was to undertake a conformance grading of a deck 12 months after installation he/she would be obliged to grade, not what is seen before him/her, but what they imagined it looked like at the time of production. That is one of the reasons there is a big difference between grading to specification and grading for fitness for purpose.

Fig. 65. Shelling out longitudinally

Fig. 66 Shelling out radially

There is one natural feature even the best grader cannot pick at the time of production and that is "shelling out". It eludes them because it is not visible at the time of production and most likely not even at the time of "sign off". Shelling out is when there is delamination between the growth rings associated with raising of the grain. This shelling out can be dangerous with bare feet.

Fig. 67 Sharp edges associated with gum vein

Sometimes a very similar effect is seen associated with gum veins and gum pockets which is why their presence should be limited in decking, When specifying an F rated product the allowance is usually very generous.

Invariably, if a piece of decking is going to shell out it will be within the first six months. If there is any likelihood of bare feet, an asset owner needs to establish, from the outset, an inspection regime to make any affected boards safe. A battery operated angle grinder will do this in seconds. Some boards will still need to be replaced. We have found that when this is an issue, generally only 2 to 3% of boards are affected. When writing the specification it should include a clause whereby after 6 months the builder has to reinspect the deck and replace any boards where shelling out is an issue.

We have observed that shelling is not an issue with decking produced from 100 x 25 mm boards. I have heard no explanation why this is so. Issues relating to gum veins are an issue in all size timber.

The Suitability of Pine for Decks/Boardwalks

Pine makes a very effective house framing timber when it is correctly treated but as decking, and even joists with heavy gauge screws, it is a totally different matter. Some years ago I was speaking with the management of a major pine mill in Queensland and asked if they made pine decking. "Yes, quite a lot," they replied but went on to say "But I cannot understand why anyone would ever use it." Success in the much milder climate of Tasmania is no guarantee of success in the Queensland heat. Conversely, if it works well in Queensland, it will excel in Tasmania.

Fig. 68. Pine self destructing in the Queensland weather.

When I started Outdoor Structures Australia in 1997 many Queensland local governments had a resistance to and some even refused to purchase hardwood for their boardwalk projects. The "greenies" were agitating and timber from environmentally friendly pine forests was seen as the way to save everything including the whale. Formal policies were even adopted to enforce this. Where are these boardwalks now? Invariably, they have been ripped out already or are so deteriorated that they need to be. The only exceptions were those that were well shaded. I have not heard that objection for some years. The asset owners found out afterwards that the 40 year warranty covered against decay and termite attack only, but excluded self destruction caused by wetting and drying.[14] For Queensland councils, this was an expensive mistake and went against all logic and conflicting environmental views.

The logic, of course, was the evidence before your eyes. Where had pine ever been used successfully in full sun in the warmer states? Also, where do you find an environmentally friendly and well managed exotic pine forest in Queensland? The "feral weed" as the hardwood industry calls slash and radiata pine, was introduced to this country. You generally only get an exotic pine forest by bulldozing a perfectly healthy hardwood forest. While city dwellers were getting their "warm fuzzies" by looking at mental pictures of a well managed pine plantation I saw only the detritus of a badly managed native hardwood forest. On more than one occasion when we were producing powerpoles we were phoned by the Department saying "Remove the poles by such and such a date as, after that, it is all going to be bulldozed and burnt." I considered the use of pine as the better environmental choice for decking was never defendable but, as always, people wanted a simplistic answer. In the place of a healthy ecosystem selectively harvested every 20 to 30 years there was now one almost devoid of native wildlife. The introduction of the South East Queensland Forests Agreement in 1989 put an end to the lie that using hardwood was unsustainable and bad.

---

[14] This is covered in more detail in the section on Warranties in my *Timber Preservation Guide*.

Fig. 69. Split 45mm pine joist.

A further complication arose as the pine joists were only available in 45 mm and not 75. I was told, "Pine joists won't split" but this Figure 69 disproves that. In my *Timber Preservation Guide* I wrote about the effectiveness of treatment in sawn pine. Briefly, if you can purchase pine incised to a depth of 8 mm and structurally graded and combined with the American *Deckmaster* system. then it should work extraordinarily well as joists in commercial decks. At the time of writing there is no manufacturer of this product in Australia.

Take Care When Using or Specifying Kwila/Merbau

If the environmental issues are not enough to cause you to rethink whether you should use kwila/merbau, tannin staining should cause you to think twice.

Environmental. There seems to be a much greater awareness in New Zealand than Australia of the environmental issues involved with using kwila/merbau. The NZ government estimates that this one species alone represents 80% of the illegally logged timber coming into that country. Is it a great stretch of the imagination to then accept that a similar situation does not exist in Australia.

All the kwila/merbau coming into the country seems to claim be certified but I am a little sceptical. While I am not saying do not use kwila/merbau, I would urge some heart searching before you specify it.[15] The slang term for it in the industry is "monkey wood".

Tannin Stains. Kwila/merbau is similar to blackbutt in that there is a large problem with tannins. Tannin staining is virtually impossible to deal with as many; if not most, clear sealants will not go straight over new kwila/merbau. Our own Tanacoat requires kwila/merbau to have at least three months weathering prior to its application. Different manufacturers ask for similar or even longer weather exposure.

One of my newsletter readers told me how some poor professional designed a second story deck where he/she specified kwila decking. Under the deck was parking for the client's two very expensive cars. The first time it rained the paintwork on the cars was so badly damaged that the designer had to pay for a repaint. Treat tannin stains seriously.

On the other hand, the Australian species with probably the least amount of staining is spotted gum.

---

[15] One wholesaler came to me trying to sell merbau and boasting how all their timber was environmentally certified. Knowing of endemic corruption in the country it was sourced from; I asked "What was value of the certificate." He said jokingly that when they approached their ten suppliers, "Nine headed for the hills and the other said, 'No problem', my uncle is a printer." Sometimes more truth is said in jest than we care to admit.

Spotted gum can be sealed immediately with Tanacoat – see Maintenance of external timber in our *Traffic Barrier, Fencing and Bollard Guide*.

Oiling Decking

When I get really frustrated I tend to break out with, "Dear Lord, give me strength". Let me tell you of a "give me strength" moment as it relates to oiling decking. CN oil is an extremely robust decking oil and is excellent to apply on decking in public applications such as decks and boardwalks. CN emulsion is a grease that is painted onto the end grain of timber. Over the years we have seen these two mixed up. We had a case where this happened on a deck on a commercial building. The painter got the grease and painted it all over the deck. Now the moment you open the can and look at its consistency something must tell you, "This is not right". If he had turned his head and had a look at the white carpet behind him, alarm bells had to ring loudly. It didn't. He just did as the plans directed without asking any questions. This painter might be working on your next job. Worrying isn't it?

We also find that some confuse the preservative we used, Tanalith E, with a surface coating. Table 1 explains the difference between the different products we sold. The table has cautionary notes.

Tanalith E Preservative Outdoor Structures Australia did not use any CCA in its decks or substructure except for high risk H5 in ground structural applications. Our products complied with the APVMA guidelines for the use of treated timber. All preservatives may be significantly enhanced by additional coatings to minimise weathering.

GUIDE TO USING THE CORRECT SURFACE COATING		
CN OIL	**CN EMULSION**	**TANACOAT**
CN Oil is an extremely robust oil with additional preservatives. Generally it used as the first oil coat on external decking. It is intended for commercial decks where the users are walking onto concrete or natural earth. CN Oil can be applied in our factory. **IMPORTANT** **CN Oil is not suitable for domestic or commercial applications** where people may walk onto carpets or other surfaces that might stain. It should not be used on handrails.	CN Emulsion is a grease like timber preservative that is applied liberally to end-grain and timber to timber interfaces. It is also applied to the top of the dampcourses under the decking. **IMPORTANT** CN Emulsion should not be confused with CN Oil and should never be applied to the face of the timber.	Tanacoat is penetrating timber oil. It is not as robust as CN Oil and is not a preservative. This oil works as a UV blocker and water repellent. A typical application is re-oiling of existing decks. Decks coated originally with CN oil should be aged for three months before applying Tanacoat. Tanacoat should also be used when dripping of CN oil can be an issue. It should be the first coat when people walk from the deck onto carpet etc. Tanacoat is suitable for handrails. Tanacoat can not be applied in the factory.[16] **IMPORTANT** Waxy species such as kwila/murbau and tallowwood should be aged three months before application.
Check that you have specified and are using the coatings correctly		

Table 1. Correct coating guides

---

[16] At the time of writing Infrastrucxion Pty. Ltd., a licensee to Outdoor Structures IP, has ordered a new spray booth to make this possible. Reader should enquire about the current state of availability.

Use of Different Joist Material

Decking on Steel Joists

| Fig. 70. Fixings breaking in C section steel. | Fig. 71. Corroding C section joists, Image courtesy of Contrast Constructions. |

How would you like to spend $250,000 to replace a ten year old deck, disgraceful enough in itself, only to find that the screws are breaking and you have trip hazards on the deck? What about having your steel joists corrode in a relatively short time? These are real, but fortunately avoidable, problems associated with steel joists.

When we wrote our *LifePlus Decking Guide* in 2004 we realised that many people wanted to put their domestic decking on steel joists as they thought this would avoid the problems that can be associated with timber subframes. We experience the same with commercial decking as well. The problems with timber joists are well known and can all be designed around if you are prepared to take a little care. We explained how to do that with domestic decking in the *LifePlus guide* and for commercial decking in our *Deckwood Selection Guide*. We had no objections to using steel for joists but realised that the builder was swapping well known and solvable problems for problems that were less understood. At the time we wrote to Bluescope Lysaghts outlining what we saw would be the problems and asking how to design around them. The difficulties we saw were:

- Increased corrosion protection is needed especially with new treatment chemicals[17]
- Lipped profiles allow moisture to pool
- Lower torsional stiffness of C and Z sections than hardwood
- Screw fixings breaking when used in steel joists.

After about two years we finally received a verbal reply. We were told that Bluescope Lysaghts

---

[17] See the discussion in my *Timber Preservation Guide*.

provided no warranty when their steel was used with external timber. This was because there is associated moisture which causes corrosion. You will find a similar statement in the Bluescope 2006 publication *Corrosion Technical Bulletin CTB 13*. That would be the end of the matter except that the Lysaght publication *Construction of a Lysaght QuickaFloor*[18] outlines how to make a verandah floor with their product and does not appear to mention that you are not to use timber decking. A phone call indicated that decking would have to be screwed or nailed with a hardened twisted shank nail as with the internal floor sheeting instructions. A publication I personally found more helpful was the *Duragal Flooring System* published by Onesteel.[19] Their guide gives design solutions for all the issues I sought guidance on, which includes the use of Norton Flashtack as a dampcourse.

By all means use steel joists but going to steel does not solve the problem of needing to take great care, perhaps even more care in detailing and construction. Contact the joist supplier to get their written recommendations.

When I looked at that job with the broken screws it made me wonder why we use timber at all until we understand that plastic decking would have been worse. Tragically, the asset owner will probably go to plastic next time thinking they had solved the problem only to find they had taken on a whole host of problems they had not expected.

---

[18] Viewed at http://www.lysaght.com/files/dmfile/QuikaFloorConstructionGuidejune07.pdf . Date accessed, 13 June 2012. I have been advised that this document is to be revised in light of my comments. Refer to later editions.
[19] Viewed at http://www.onesteel.com/images/db_images/productspecs/DFS%20Brochure.pdf. Date accessed, 30 June 2012.

Decking on LVL or Laminated Beams

Fig. 72. H3 treated LVL that started failing after 18 months. Image courtesy of Alex Fleri, Original Decking.

When sawing timber for logs sourced under the forest agreements it is much easier to produce the decking than the joists. In a moment of weakness I contemplated using LVL's as this would have simplified our business substantially. Wiser heads cautioned, "Ted, that's not a good idea. The 14 gauge screws [used with commercial decking] will split them open". We see in Figure 72 the consequence of gun nailing (only 2.5mm not the 6 mm screw) domestic decking straight onto H3 treated LVL's. There were no dampcourses or emulsions but it is doubtful if it would have been a long term fix as the LVL's, which are laminated vertically, would still have split and, at best, the nails would have worked out and possibly cut feet open. The replacement joists used were finger jointed and laminated H3 LOSP (light organic solvent preservative) pine with a dampcourse and coated with CN Oil. The decking was screwed down with 10 gauge screws.

It is tempting to consider using a treated laminated beam where greater spans are required especially considering their lightness in pine. Timber does not rust so could easily be considered ideal for a marine environment as well.

The problem with the Australian manufactured beams in our Queensland conditions is that the timber can quickly delaminate due to the effect of wetting and drying and UV. Fasteners are often screwed directly into the girders and so there can be deterioration of the beam itself. The effect is much less in colder climates. It is not that the deterioration does not occur, it just takes longer.

Fig. 73. Delamination of hardwood laminated beam.

OSA's practice when a weather exposed laminated beam had to be used was to accommodate the product's limitations. The beam we would use would normally be made from pine with the individual laminates LOSP treated prior to laminating. Painting with CN (copper napthenate) oil is also a good practice. The outer beam would be shielded with a set of timber louvers that protect from rain and UV. Using the maximum possible overhang on the decking also helps.

Fig. 74. Weathering louvers on side of beam.

Fig. 75. Bolting rail fastened to the side of the beams.

The decking would not be fastened directly into the beams. Figure 75 shows the use of ex 100x100 mm bolting rails that are fastened to the sides of the beams These rails have a sloping top to direct rainwater away from the beam. A folded aluminium dampcourse was added to the top of the beam. This particular structure was designed for a small fire truck to cross which required heavy 70 mm decking and was bolted (not screwed) from the top.

Even with this extra attention we would never have used these beams above Bundaberg. By comparison, laminated beams are available overseas with very robust treatments and with cyclic delamination resistant glues. This makes them a logical choice for many applications. At the time of writing, beams of this calibre are not manufactured in Australia. I am aware that some are being imported for specialty products such as bridge girders by Timber Restoration Systems.

Decking on Fibre Composite Joists

Fig. 76 Deck frame in fibre composites

Fig. 77. Cross section of joist

There is a misguided belief that timber is suitable only for temporary structures and that, for a modern structure to succeed, it must be constructed using modern material such as fibre composite joists. Now we are aware that this product appears to make excellent crossarms on powerpoles but what about deck and boardwalk joists? The jury is still out on that subject but I have no real objections to their use as such. But remember, you are swapping the well known and easily solvable problems of one material for the lesser known problems of another. Let me explain.

We had a customer in a quandary late in 2012. He was using our Deckwood with fibre composite joists. The contractors had made a test panel and found that the screws stripped out easily if they had to exert the extra pressure needed to straighten the boards. How crooked were the boards? They were within Australian Standards guidelines and when I stood on them they went straight. (Now I have to admit that I weigh more than I should). The problem was not the boards but the thin wall thickness of the joist (Figure 77). Installing subsequent boards on the test panel, as in a re-decking situation, caused problems also. This was due to the difficulties caused by drilling holes close to or intersecting existing holes. Remember, these joists are supposed to be a 100 year life product which means 4 decks. This in turn means that the top will look like Swiss cheese. We suggested to the client that a simple solution would be to use H4 treated Ironwood pine by CHH (No substitution. Read my timber preservation guide to find out why not) and screw into the pine as well.

There are situations where the use of fibre composite joists makes complete sense such as where access is difficult and its lightness is an essential. There are others where it does not. A correctly detailed and more economical high durability hardwood joist has a design life of 85 years and are we going to argue the toss over 15 years when the job will probably be redone well beforehand?

Common Design Issues

Changes of direction

| Fig. 78. Sinuous path achieved with tapered Deckwood. | Fig. 79. Use of a trimmer at sharp angles. Note long pointed ends. |

Changing direction on boardwalks and decks can be more complicated than it first appears. When using a simple mitre, the difficulties are in:

- Controlling long pointed decking ends at the intersection
- Achieving a neat mitre.

Long pointed ends on decking can be dangerous as they tend to rise and have the potential to give a nasty (and very expensive) spearing injury. This detail should be avoided at all costs but is frequently found.

Changes Up to 13 Degrees

Outdoor Structures Australia normally avoided both these problems by the use of tapered decking. We used our standard tapered Deckwood for changes of direction up to 13 degrees per pile bent and for sharper angles we used mitre incorporating a trimmer as illustrated in Figure 79. This requires extra detailing in the subframe. We produced standard tapered Deckwood segments that were 90 mm at one end and 60 mm on the other. Their length needed to be at least 50 mm longer than the nominal width of the Boardwalk and ideally 300 mm. In Table 2 the number of segments needed for each 10 degree change of direction is shown.

Nom. width	segments required	Nom. width	segments required
1.2	8 approx	2.1	13 approx
1.5	9 approx	2.4	15 approx
1.8	11 approx		
Table 2. Segments per 10 degrees			

A method we have found satisfactory when working with tapers is to work from the centre of the angle, placing deckers equally each side of the centre. The large end of the proprietary tapers is cut square, so place these in such a manner that a neat radius is formed. Fix with two screws at the large end and one screw on each other joist. Trim the narrow end. It may be necessary to adjust the rate of the change in direction by inserting some parallel sided deckers or even inserting some tapers the other way around. Remember that the shrinkage will be different at each end and you will need to specify something like "Lay with a 3mm gap at the small end and touching at the large end".

Fig. 80. Laying tapered decking.

Fig. 81. Ends too small to be structural. Note screw positions.

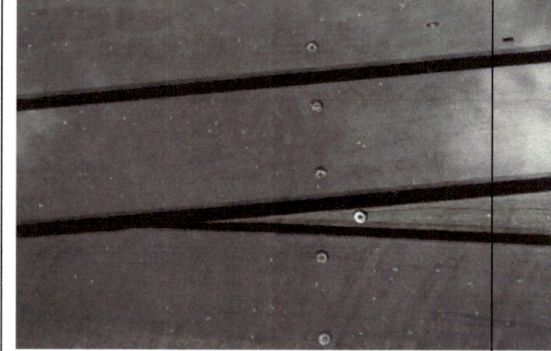

Fig. 82. Sharp end also note screw position

It is necessary to be very clear when specifying tapers, saying something like "Standard Outdoor Structures tapers @ XYZ length" and not leave it to the imagination of the builder as the small end tends to be cut too fine. They should not be less than 60 mm at the small end and have virtually clear timber.

Changes More Than 13 Degrees

Fig. 83. Unrestrained sharp end.

If a mitred joint is to be used, be aware that the designer has to detail the mitre so it is safe as well as neat. Neatness is virtually impossible without a trimmer. For the mitres to work accurately the pile bent must be exactly mid angle in the change of direction or the mitres will not match. It is safer to assume they will not match and have the deckers align with a trimmer and so hide any misalignment. As mentioned, a long tapered cut will result which tends to lift and become a spearing hazard. As part of the working drawings a detail must be included to show the acceptable method of building the taper. The ends of the joists need to be trimmed between with 75 mm minimum material and a piece of 150x50 mm fitted horizontally between the joist trimmers to support the decking trimmer. Dampcourse is set in place and the decking trimmer is secured on top and the decking screwed down at the pointed end as well. This is definitely not best practice for screw positioning but safety overrides any other consideration.

Very Sharp Changes of Direction

A 180 degree change in direction is easy to achieve with a simple return end and there are no tapers or pointed ends to be concerned with. Sharp curves can be accommodated by using short segments around an arc. The problem with pointed ends still has to be addressed. Refer to our *Boardwalk Selection Guide* as to minimum curves that are allowed with bikeways. Check also if there is any machinery, such as golf course mowers, that will use the path and can it traverse the deck?

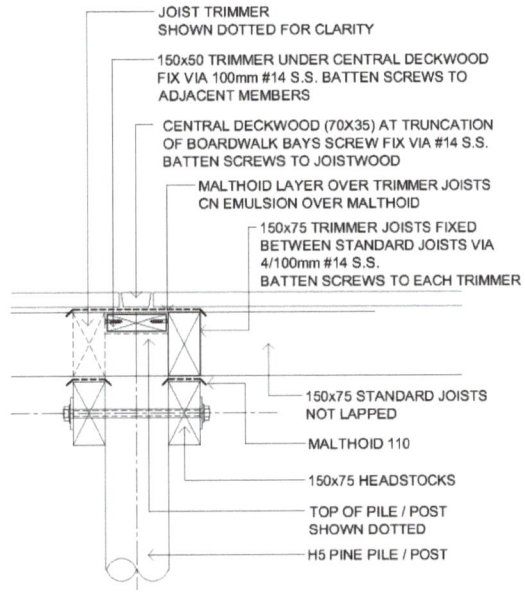

Fig. 84. Detail of trimmer joist.

Decking Gaps

Fig. 85. I had no trouble finding gaps of this size.	Fig. 86. One of my readers was injured by this 29mm gap.
Gaps in a Prominent Deck in Canberra	

In early 2005 I was sent a set of plans from which to quote the materials for a prominent deck in Canberra. As I looked at these plans I could see that this deck should not be built as originally drawn. The aesthetics were stunning but, in the transition from architectural intent to working drawings and specification, there were some serious issues. The main problem I saw was that the design utilised wide unseasoned decking laid **with** a gap. After seasoning, the gaps had to well exceed that which is considered safe for the public. I wrote to the engineers and offered my assistance to make this high profile deck a success but, unfortunately, it was declined.

In 2009 I was visiting Canberra and decided to see how the deck had performed in its transition from paper to real life. Of course, the mathematics are so basic that it had not only to fail the disability code, but fail it by a long way. I had no trouble finding gaps of 24 mm! I thought about whether I should say something to the asset owner, (that is what duty of care would demand) but then, against my better judgment, decided that no one would listen or care.

Unfortunately, one of my newsletter readers contacted me a little while later to say that he, or more accurately his bike, had found an even wider gap! Over the handlebars he went, stitches to the face and damage to his back. Tragically, no one would talk to me at the design stage when all that was needed were a few simple changes to make the deck meet basic safety standards. Now there is a continuing danger that the asset owner will be forced to talk to a solicitor acting for injured users. The old adage from medicine, "First, do no harm" applies to decking design also. I have seen enough pain in my life and would do all that is in my power to prevent anyone experiencing it unnecessarily. We all should. As for the deck, it remains the same. No one listens or cares even after paying compensation to my reader.

The following will guide you through the issues that are involved in delivering a safer deck.

Maximum Gaps: Clauses from codes relating to gaps that you need to consider when designing decks are:

Part 13 of Austroads (which quotes from the Disability Code) section 2.1.4 which covers drainage and grated areas. These can only have a maximum opening of 13 mm wide and 150 mm long to prevent entrapment of wheel chairs and walking sticks

Part 14 of Austroads section 8.5.1, grooves (and presumably even more so with gaps) are not to exceed 12 mm when parallel to travel. Refer table 8-1 of Austroads.

So if you are designing a deck you need to aim for a gap no bigger than 12 to 13 mm[20]. How do you do this with unseasoned timber? There are four steps.

1. Set your target gap

2. Nominate your species. You should be specifying Deckwood by Infrastrucxion as spotted gum and ironbark in the appropriate grades are excellent decking timbers. They only shrink 6%. If you just say something vague like F14 hardwood Above-Ground Durability Class 1 or 2, you can be dealing with up to 12% shrinkage! We do not recommend specifying Blackbutt which is very commonly done in NSW. Our Deckwood takes care of all this for you.

3. Deduct your expected shrinkage from the target gap and that is your laying gap. If you have a minus figure then you have a problem! You will have to adjust the decking width or be forced to use seasoned material.

4. Ensure the builders straighten the boards as they lay them. A piece of 150x50 decking 4.0m long supplied to AS2082 can have spring of 18 mm. This plays havoc with your gaps.

Fig. 87. Straightening decking to control gaps

As a rule of thumb, do not go above 145 mm wide unseasoned decking. If you lay without a gap your expected shrinkage with spotted gum is 9 mm. That leaves you 3 mm tolerance for spring or for areas where the boards are undersize. You will never make an ex 200 mm wide unseasoned decking fully comply with the codes, even with lower shrinkage species. We only used these wider boards on vehicle bridge decks.

---

[20] I have heard of cases where the health and safety officer has come along to a completed boardwalk and measured every gap!

Inappropriate Footwear: Figure 88 should fix in our minds how critical it is to design decking gaps correctly. A public venue has different requirements from a bush track. While referring above to 12 or 13 mm maximum gap to meet different codes, this maximum gap is far too big for situations where high heels can be expected. We might speak of inappropriate footwear but rather it is really a matter of inappropriate gaps.

I once had a phone call from a solicitor who had found our information on the web. She was acting for a woman who had her high heel caught in an alleged 12 mm gap and broke her ankle in two places! This is messy as 12 mm is within the codes. I referred her to a forensic engineer I knew. A 12 mm gap and 4 mm stiletto heels do not mix (yes, it does happen). We were asked by an architect for assistance designing a deck for a university campus club where it was expected that high heels would be regularly worn. In that case we used 70x35 mm Deckwood laid without a gap. The expected gap (shrinkage) was only 4.2 mm. Feedback from the architect confirmed that this has been a success and so we repeated it in other university situations. The gap can be designed and controlled.

Fig. 88. High heels and wide gaps do not go together.

We normally aimed for about a 7 mm gap and there is no need to exceed 9 mm except on vehicle decks, and this is with unseasoned timber.

Seasoned or unseasoned: If you want a very narrow gap (3 mm say) it simply has to be seasoned but, in practice, the majority of decking does not need so narrow a gap and so can, and should be, supplied unseasoned. The difference between using seasoned over unseasoned is:

- more expense
- more delays
- usually poorly specified (I cannot overstress this point),
- not available from anything thicker than ex 50mm
- and most importantly
- lots and lots of green house gases are needed (17 to 19 MJ per m^3 required to dry hardwood).

By automatically writing KD for the decking, the designer does not have to think too hard but at the cost of not mastering the medium that he/she is working in. We also need to be consistent in our thinking. If we are not climate change deniers, and we only boil just enough water to make the required amount of tea/coffee because it is a responsible environmental choice, then there should always be heart searching before specifying KD on anything over ex 25 mm thick. The shrinkage is known through correct species specification and by correct detailing, the resultant shrinkage can be designed around. The sun will dry the timber for free without creating any greenhouse gasses. I believe strongly that any timber structure that is unnecessarily kiln dried should not qualify for green points but I would be a voice crying in the wilderness.

One of the things kiln drying doesn't do is remove the tannins. Only exposure to the weather does this.

One of my newsletter readers asked me to share with designers a concern about decking gaps and seasoned timber that is easily overlooked. Too narrow a gap can be as big an issue as too big a gap. I have copied his words almost exactly:

Fig. 89. Decking without a gap is a safety hazard. Image courtesy Colin Mackenzie.

Just back from a week's holiday. At the Bunya Mountains, the rental house we stayed in had a timber deck, about 135 mm cover. Boards were hard butted together and no gap to allow water to drain. It was probably laid with a gap originally but in this moist rainforest environment, boards expanded and stayed expanded. When we had the storm last week you can see from the pics that the water just ponded and was still ponded the next day. Another issue was, because the deck stays wet for a long time, green mould had occurred on the surface and is as slippery as an ice skating rink when wet and very dangerous. I reported this to the property managers because I nearly slipped badly when getting more firewood to keep warm, even knowing it was slippery.

Thought this could be a good practical topic to discuss in your newsletter. i.e. design gaps for the environment and the as laid timber MC.

If 136 mm wide timber, dried to 10% MC is put in a very moist environment and then rises to say 16%, the timber will expand over 3mm, a nail diameter, which was probably the spacer used in the first place. (Spotted gum moves 0.4% of its cross section for every 1% change in moisture content).[21] Always consider the micro environment. The same situation is a problem in rainforests as well. A narrow board would have helped here and been less expensive.

---

[21] Queensland Government, Dept of Agriculture, Fishery and Forestry, Timber Species Properties and Uses, *Spotted Gum* http://www.daff.qld.gov.au/26_5162.htm. Date Accessed 6 June 2012

Laying Deckwood on Concrete with Restricted Clearance

We have, from time to time been asked to provide solutions where Deckwood needed to be laid on an already constructed concrete deck where there is as little as 100 mm recess in concrete slab. This is despite the BCA requiring a minimum of 150 mm gap under a timber deck, (Once I was asked to quote for the design and supply of a deck at a Hong Kong University. There was a 50 mm recess! It was a lost cause.) While 100 mm is far from an ideal arrangement, unlike the 50 mm gap, it can be made to work reasonably satisfactorily. While our hardwoods do not particularly mind getting wet, they need to dry quickly and this does not happen if joists are screwed directly to the concrete. Clearance under the joists and a self-draining fall on the slab to the outside are essential.

Fig. 90. Deck built over a 100 mm recess.

Fig. 91. Support studs for joists.

Fig. 92. Joists ready for decking.

The way OSA dealt with this on one project was as follows: The joists were 100x50 Durability 1 In-Ground F17 (which were laid on their flat) sized to 45 mm. It is critical that the timber specification clearly says ***Durability 1 In-Ground*** not just Durability 1 (a designation that is discontinued but has not seemed to have worked through to many designers) as the lowest price tenderer will say "This is an above ground application so I will use a lower price Durability 1 Above-Ground timber." You must also control shrinkage to a maximum of 6% by nominating a range of acceptabl;e species, e.g. ironbark and/or tallowwood. By just specifying F14/F17 you have no idea what you are receiving. In the project illustrated, the joists were pre-drilled and countersunk at our workshop prior to delivery. The joists were laid out and the positions of the supporting studs marked. The builder then drilled into the slab and epoxied in short lengths of 12 mm, stainless threaded rod and nuts were then run down the stud. Of course, when you have a waterproof membrane, things get very complicated.

The shrinkage was then calculated (45 mm joist + 35 mm decking = 80 mm shrinkage 6% = approx 5 mm) and the nuts set to a level where the deck would be about 2.5 mm (1/2 of the shrinkage) above the adjoining concrete deck. We were able to achieve a gap of about 20-25 mm under the joist. Protruding studs were cut off and then dampcourse and CN emulsion were added to the top of the joists. Decking was then laid without a gap.

So, while it is not an ideal arrangement it can be made to work. It is much better to talk to us before designing a low clearance deck.

Notes on Hardware

Alternative Fixings

Fig. 93. Deckmaster (US) Hidden Fixing System

Fig. 94. Screwing from underneath at and angle.

When I was a young man I studied logic and I leant of an error called *the fallacy of two terms* and here we have a classic, *Deckmaster*. There are two totally different concealed fixing systems by that name. One *Deckmaster* system is a folded steel strip system from the US which attaches to the side of the joist and allows the builder to fasten from underneath.[22] It is available from Grabber Construction Products. The other *Deckmaster* is a concealed metal clip that fits into a pre-machined groove in the side of the decking and attaches to the top of the joist. This second system is marketed by Wilson Timbers who are the owner of the name *Deckmaster* in Australia.[23] Confused?

We only once had experience with the US *Deckmaster* system used in conjunction with our 120x35 unseasoned Deckwood. The domestic (not commercial) strips were available in Australia at the time in stainless steel and lightly galvanised.[24] The treatment manufacturers and Australian manufacturers of folded metal construction products recommendation is for stainless steel in this application whether coastal or not. The stainless strips were expensive but the home owner was an opening batsman for Australia so cost was not an issue. The product worked so well we received a free endorsement, quite something in the commercial world of test cricket. The arrangement of strips means that the screws are inserted at an angle giving a longer grip in the timber. While the screws were of a smaller gauge than we would normally use, they did not give problems.[25] The joist only needs to be 50 mm not 75 mm and individual boards can be replaced. The joist does not need to be seasoned.

---

[22] Refer www.deckmaster.com. Date accessed, 14 June 2012.
[23] Refer http://www.deckmaster.com.au Date accessed, 14 June 2012.
[24] The US *Deckmaster* site now lists powdercoated strips which are ACQ compliant but would not be suitable within 10K of the coast if we follow the Arch and Pryda's recommendation.
[25] We oiled the deck twelve months after installation so we had an opportunity to see its actual performance.

Note: I am of the opinion that this system, combined with horizontal bolting will give the maximum life to a timber structure. Unfortunately, at the time of writing, this is not available in Australia to my knowledge.

Fig. 95. Any damage at the corner becomes important with grooved decking. Image courtesy of Alex Fleri of Original Decking.

The Australian *Deckmaster* is a face fixed steel clip[26] of sophisticated design which should perform better than the plastic biscuits often seen advertised. It is only new on the market at the time of writing so we cannot say much about its long term performance in Australian hardwoods. Our observation is that when 19mm decking is machined with a side groove there is not much timber above the groove. This makes it more susceptible to damage. Ideally, a thicker board with more material above the groove would be desirable. The clips and biscuits can only be used on seasoned or very low shrinkage timber. Heavier *Deckmaster* clips are available for use in commercial decking. We looked closely at them but could not make them work on our tapered side decking.

A system we are about to trial at the time of writing is a timber dowel system. It comes highly recommended by a person whose judgement I trust. The dowels are stepped and a hole is drilled with a bit with matching steps. The dowel has glue added and is driven into place. This system has been used successfully in the US where there is a wide range of climates just like Australia, and on dense hardwoods such as Ipe. Both the decking and the joist have to be seasoned so domestic KD hardwood on treated pine joists would work. These dowels will be available through Infrastrucxion Pty Ltd if trials are satisfactory.

Fig. 96. Dowel fastenings.

---

[26] It is said to be yet another product developed in Australia that had to go offshore to be manufactured.

Volute Washers, a Useful Piece of Hardware

Fig. 97 Volute washer.

Many designers are not aware of a very useful item of hardware for timber engineering called a volute washer. I first became aware of them many years ago when I was producing power poles and crossarms. These washers were used on pole hardware to take up the shrinkage in unseasoned timber so retightening would not be needed over a 30 year service life. These washers will take up about 25 mm of shrinkage. On our bridges we used them on our timber handrail posts and under large kerbs (125x125 and bigger). Attention to detail like this meant it is very difficult to be the lowest tenderer.

The volute washer is a coil of 6 mm approx stainless spring steel wire that compresses within itself. It is available in a range of sizes to suit 12, 16, 20 and 24 mm bolts. The volute washer needs a square washer under the nut. When we used them on a painted surface we used a large square washer under the volute washer itself to prevent damage to the paint. With the brand we purchased, the m12/16 washer measured approx 65 mm across and about 30 mm in height and the m20/24 washer measures 85x35 mm. Remember that you need longer bolts.

Malthoid a Mixed Blessing

Fig. 98. Boardwalk by OSA with Malthoid on top of joists and CN emulsion on top of the Malthoid

Fig. 99. Area around vertical through bolt where Malthoid held water next to the wood bearer causing the cross bearers to decay in 8 years Image courtesy Dan Tingly

Fig. 100. An 8 year old deck and cross bearers removed due to decay in bearers with Malthoid still showing. Image courtesy Dan Tingley, Wood Research and Development

As previously mentioned, we had taken a "belt and braces" approach to ensuring maximum joist life in our Boardwalks. The "belt" is to fully predrill for the screws in a staggered alignment. (We recommended staggering a minimum of 8 mm either side of the centre line thus forcing a minimum 75 mm joist be used). The "braces" was the use of Malthoid dampcourse so, if there is any minor splitting, moisture does not enter the joist and cause decay. We had been recommending Malthoid as the dampcourse for the sole reason that it is more reasonably priced than other dampcourses. Our practice was to place the Malthoid on the joist after all other construction has been completed but just prior to laying the deck. The Malthoid went directly against the joist and a liberal coat of CN emulsion was added to the top of the Malthoid. The emulsion worked as a water repellent between the dampcourse and the decking. The deck is then secured with 14# stainless screws.

Note: When using lapped joists ensured that the dampcourse covered both joists and no moisture can enter between the two.

With this method of construction there are no oversize holes for bolts going through the Malthoid, only undersize screw holes and the tar in the Malthoid should have sealed around these. Our initial experience was that the dampcourse seals the top of the joist so well that you may even have to chip it off to remove it. This adhesion happened very quickly as there is no movement in the joists to speak of. Because it appeared so effective in boardwalks I had come to see it as a panacea for all ills and the mental jump to using it on all timber structures is a logical one.

It was drawn to my attention by Prof. Dan Tingley at the 2011 Small Bridge Conference that the use of Malthoid in road bridges is actually counterproductive. Here its use can be very different to that on boardwalks as **oversize** holes pass through the dampcourse unlike with the screws which are **undersize**.

These oversize holes allow moisture to pass through and sit between the Malthoid and the item it is meant to protect. This promotes rather than delays degrade. This effect is compounded as with all the movement in a vehicle bridge you do not get the adhesion to the timber that you find in a boardwalk. The dampcourse itself is also likely to degrade with the movement.

As I started to investigate further I found that with the imported material we were no longer getting the adhesion to the joists that I found with the earlier Australian made product. But I also found that after 10 years the product seemed to be working in boardwalks in the Brisbane locality. But investigations with councils in northern Queensland (tropical and with high rainfall) revealed that decay was promoted with the use of Malthoid. I also observed that when boards were replaced the dampcourse was damaged and would have retained moisture.

So after years of advising the use of Malthoid dampcourse I have had to rethink the situation. For most applications, which have not been in tropical conditions the dampcourse probably has worked as required, but as a blanket advice I would say do not use Malthoid. An alternate product that I have heard good reports about is Norton Flashtack. This is the product also specified for use on steel joists by One Steel. It most likely works better than Malthoid. The bituminised finish is important to seal the screw. The vinyl joist strips do not do this.

Headstock Bolts Used with Natural Rounds

When dealing with turned pine posts, the diameters are even which makes ordering the bolts very simple as every one will be exactly the same size. This is not the case with natural rounds. The size varies dramatically. In the project illustrated in Fig. ? the piles varied from 300mm to 420mm. As the bolts were custom made stainless steel all the one length, (I expect to suit 300mm), the amount of the check varied from slight to excessive. The one holds moisture much more than the other.

Fig. 101. Incorrect bolt length means large checkouts on the post top.

It is better to allow for the variation in size of the natural rounds by using threaded rod cut to length on site. It would also be a lot less expensive. But if at all possible a checkout should be avoided, and in this case, it would have been easier to fit a large heart in bearer across the tops of the piles and fasten without any vertical through bolts.

Some Case Histories

Australian Examples

This guide is filled with images of problem decks in Australia. With most of them I have not disclosed the location out of tact. There are two Australian examples, one that is desperately wrong and the other is as good as it is possible to build a deck.

Specifications Should Mean Something

Fig. 102. An attempted copy of an OSA bedlog boardwalk

The recession following the GFC left me very frustrated over the pointlessness of specifications being written by professional designers. There is no value putting effort into the design and putting professional indemnity at risk if no attempt is made to determine if what is supplied matches what is specified.

As things got harder, substitution became more blatant and some diverged even further from the nominated specification than I could have ever imagined. At the design stage many of our readers came to us for free advice, assistance and technical expertise and we got sick at heart when we saw what actually got built and how much of the certainty in the original specification has gone.

The image above is a good example of what happens when contractors substitute and purchase on price. The differences between an OSA Boardwalk (which was specified) and the boardwalk actually built are listed in Table 3 below.

Requirement to be Equal to an OSA Boardwalk	OSA	Other
Durability 1 In-Ground bedlog	Yes	Unknown
Anti split Plate for bedlog	Yes	No
CN Emulsion on bedlog	Yes	Do not think so
Royal species hardwood joist	Yes	I do not believe so
Dampcourse (overhanging) on joists	Yes	No
Royal species decking	Yes	I do not believe so
Timber to Deckwood Specification	Yes	29 out of 231 pieces not to OSA standard
Self cleaning decking	Yes	No
Oiled all round with CN Oil prior to construction	Yes	No
Kerb compliant with disability code	Yes	I do not believe so
Stainless Screws	Yes	Yes
Good ventilation	Yes	No
Stainless bolts (required for the location)	Yes	No
Construction guide supplied by manufacturer	Yes	No
Lowest cost	No	Yes

Table 3. Comparison of specification to supply.

We initially provided drawings to the client. These drawings were used in the tender document which showed the boardwalk sitting on top of the ground. The builder has constructed it with the ground level virtually at the level of the deck. The boardwalk is therefore sitting in a trough. When I performed the burning splinter test on slivers from the deck and joists it indicated that blackbutt was used. The defects in the deck are also similar to those of blackbutt. This is very likely what you will receive when you just specify F14 or F17 hardwood and purchase on price. It is a virtually meaningless specification. Remember that while this species may be suitable for bridge decking when it has a bitumen running/protective surface, it is not approved for critical weather exposed applications such as bridge substructures, crossarms and railway sleepers. Yet somehow there is an expectancy it will work in a boardwalk and especially one that is in a very demanding situation.

What is the most upsetting part of this project is that had we been involved at the supply stage we would have taken the client by the hand and advised him not to build it at all. Building in a trough is not an appropriate application for a timber boardwalk and would have been better in concrete! Down the years it is quite possible that someone will look at what must be unsatisfactory performance of this structure and make a policy decision not to build in timber again. I cannot say I would blame them.

The point of all this is that a specification should mean something! At the end of 2011, a substitution I saw was 88x20 mm pine decking used instead of our 120x35 mm Deckwood decking for a 5 kPa, 4.5 kN application. For only the third time in 14 years I complained and of course it fell on deaf ears. What happens when someone rides a horse or a quad bike on the thin pine deck? There is, after all, meant to be a point to specifications. Who is supposed to check that what is specified is actually supplied and who bears the liability if someone sues?

Calypso Bay Marina, as Good as it Gets.

Fig. 103 Calypso Bay Marina, Jacobs Well.

The Calypso Bay Marina at Jacobs Well (constructed 2004) with a 450 m long and 7.5 m wide deck was the largest order we were ever involved with. It is an excellent example of good design, supply and construction. The interaction among all the professionals on this job was outstanding. I found this job particularly satisfying as the designers said to me, "Ted, show us how it is done." The deck is constructed over salt water with no shade. There is no harder an application yet it is performing well. I cannot think of a better example of a well detailed deck.

This project demonstrates the foolishness of skimping on money at the design stage. The danger is to look up yellow pages and to ring around and get three prices, accept the lowest price and receive the first answer that is mathematically correct. Extra time spent by a specialist just thinking about how to minimise cost is the best money ever spent. Through our consultant we quoted $5500 to design this deck with 260 piles. They were purchased at what was in 2004 considered a bargain price of $650 each. By not taking extra thought, an alternative/inexperienced designer could have incurred the owner the following:

- Increasing the number of piles needed by 10 % adding $16,900
- Used 45 mm decking instead of 35 mm which would have added $140,000 and
- Longer screws needed alone would cost an extra $8000

The marina adopted all the standard OSA project features such as preoiled Deckwood decking and Joistwood joists. Fittings were stainless steel and edge clearances were maintained. Dampcourses and emulsions were standard. An unusual aspect of this design was using a 300x200 mm heart centre bearer to allow a deck about 4.8 m wide to be built without the need of second row of piles. This made piling simple (no misalignment problems) and much less expensive. The decking was clamped prior to screwing to control the gaps.

Fig. 104. Replacing pile with large bearer.

We encountered a problem with this deck. Our specification for Deckwood at that stage allowed for Forest Red Gum (FRG) as one of the species allowed and there was some FRG in the deck. We had had over 50 years' satisfactory experience with locally grown trees when used in products such as steps. FRG is a Durability 1 In-Ground Species. We sourced the timber for this deck away from the Lockyer Valley and the "foreign" FRG did not perform as expected. Many (about 2% of a very large total) pieces "shelled out" and we had to replace them. No other company would. We modified the Deckwood Selection Guide to remove any reference to FRG. It remains suitable for joists due to its durability.

Just referring to Australian Standards to base your specification is fraught with dangers. By just ticking the boxes about durability ratings etc. there is no guarantee that the product will perform well. It also opens you up to the worst possible extremes of product substitution. The genuine Deckwood product gives you years of fine tuning the specification.

International Examples

Noah's Ark in Hong Kong

Fig. 105. Reconstruction of Noah's Ark in the New Territories of Hong Kong.

Fig. 106. Associated boardwalk in a shaded section.

Fig. 107. The same boardwalk in full sun.

To the theologically minded, you might have thought that Noah and his ark came to rest on the top of Mt. Ararat. But here it is in Hong Kong! Don't worry, it is only a theme park built around a replica based on the sizes given in Genesis. This modern Noah used fibreglass for his ark and fencing instead of gopher wood. But adjoining the ark, at Ma Wan Nature Garden, and part of the overall project, is a timber boardwalk and deck built at the same time. In late 2005 we met with a representative of the developer and were asked to price the supply of that boardwalk. As I looked at the drawings again, unfortunately, there were serious issues. Concrete, steel and glass are more what you would associate with Hong Kong so it was not a surprise. The foundations were, in our opinion, over designed with heavy galvanized T sections 150x150x10 mm at close centres. What was actually built appeared to be heavier still, UC (200 mm I think). Galvanised steel corrodes in contact with the ground and concrete and the steel should have had (and were specified to have in the drawings we were shown) a corrosion resistant paint applied. It was not done. There was no obvious corrosion at the ground line yet but it will happen. There was room for substantial legitimate savings with the foundations but they certainly will not fail in a hurry. The problem was the superstructure, which we considered to be under designed, especially for Hong Kong's climate. It was built from CCA pine (no environmental issues in Hong Kong) on 50 mm joists with small 10# screws holding the decking down.

I advised the executive that they really needed to look at building some certainty into the super structure and that there would be no net increase in cost if the deck was upgraded and the foundations downgraded. I realized that we were not communicating as my comments about, "How long will it last?" would always be deflected by his "How much will it cost?" Of course the order went to someone who would claim to supply what was drawn without question and, I suggest, understanding.

In November 2010, I visited Hong Kong and decided to have a look at how the boardwalk was performing. The park was opened in July 2007 so what I saw was probably no more than three and a half years old. As I walked on the deck I thought I would have to eat humble pie (yet again) because the deck was in excellent order but then I walked out of the shade onto the large areas of the deck in full sun. There, the deck was behaving as we had advised with early degrade starting to occur. In a few years the deck will look very sad indeed.

This project reminded me of the extreme challenges in designing and building timber structures that are situated in full sun. There is no forgiveness of errors. But when the structure is under shade you can "get away with" less than best practice. To its credit, this deck does not have a kerb which would have trapped leaf litter so remains relatively clean which is a great help.

Fig. 108. Protruding screw is very dangerous.

Figure 108 from the same boardwalk shows how critical attention to detail is. The screw on the step is very close to the end and so has split the stair stringer and worked its way out about 10 mm. Imagine the financial repercussions if a wealthy American tourist trips on that, falls down the steps and breaks a hip? An over designed foundation is worth nothing then. The success of these structures always depends on getting a myriad of small details correct. The drawings we saw had a very reasonable and safe detail with galvanized brackets on a steel stringer with screws going into the step from underneath. Perhaps plans were not followed. There has to be a lesson in this.

Boardwalks for Singapore National Parks

Fig. 109. Sungei Buloh Wetlands Reserve in 2003

In about 2000 I gave a presentation on boardwalks for the Singapore National Parks. In the discussion afterwards one of their officers said to me "I don't know where the tenderers get their prices from. It's like they pluck them out of the sky." Soon after our timber was requested (despite our design information not being looked at) for a large boardwalk and we went to see the successful tenderer. He hadn't done as much as a material takeoff; in fact, it was so bad that he didn't understand the concept of ordering timber in set lengths. I asked how they arrived at a price. He said, "Oh we never bother estimating off the plans, we assess the project and come to a conclusion of what the tender will be let for and submit that price". The obvious question was how do you make a profit? He maintained that the drawings are generally always so bad that they have to be reworked before they could be built. They just kept enough of the original design to prevent the job going out to retender. All these changes were variations that bumped the price up and up. They had even been able to even double the price this way. A few dollars spent with our Australian consultant to have a design that needed no changes would be money very well spent. In the end that builder substituted who knows what for our Deckwood.

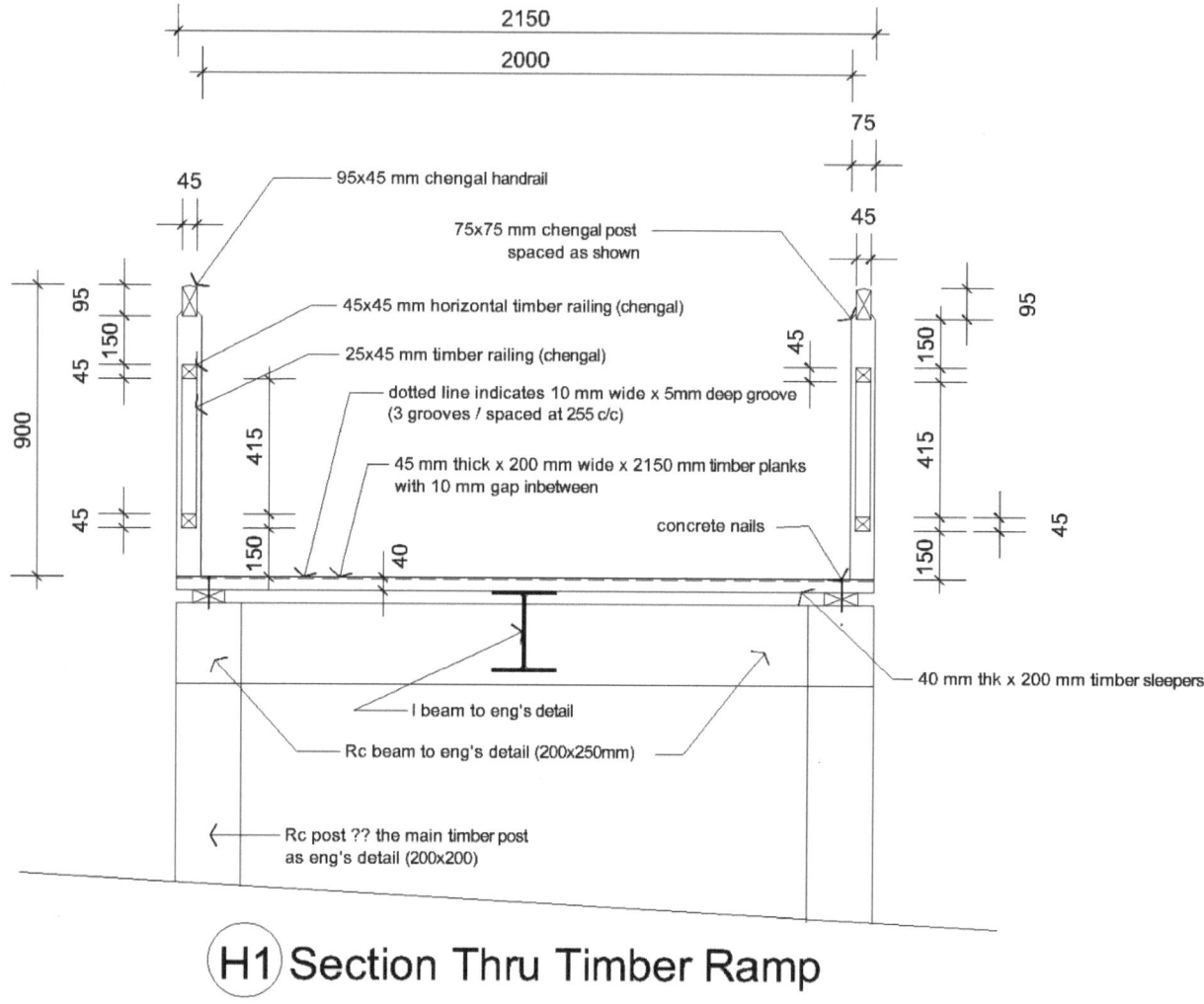

Fig. 110. Cross section through Hindhede boardwalk (redrawn from fax).

We were involved with trying to supply four boardwalks to Singapore National Parks, each of which was either unable to be built, or shouldn't have been built without serious modification. That was then and we can only hope that a different culture permeates the Board now. Saying that a boardwalk shouldn't be built without major modification is strong but consider Figure 110 . It shows a cross section of the boardwalk proposed for Hindhede Nature Park. We were not able to find any other drawings with the tender document despite the drawing saying to refer to engineer's drawings. So something that might be intended to reflect architectural intent became part of the tender documents. Some of the problems were:

- No connection of posts to joists
- Handrail post sits on top of deck without any brackets
- Decks are simply nailed through into concrete joists
- No connection detail for centre steel joist
- No centre fasteners to deck
- Handrail is only 45x45 mm.

We would not even consider supplying against these details and submitted a price based on new drawings. Others apparently saw no problems with the original drawings and were successful. Looking at images of the boardwalk on the internet, I see that the Board paid for variations but still left some of the design problems. I showed this image a little while later during a presentation at Sentosa Island in Singapore and one of the senior executives laughed, confessing that they had just built a boardwalk like the one illustrated. The builder just screwed the posts onto the deck as nothing different was drawn. Still the message did not get through about the need to deal with competent specialists.

If you get "caught" on a project you should only get caught once. There was no excuse for continuing similar practices. Not dealing with informed specialists simply isn't wise. Not all specialists are informed.

Decks at Marinoa in Fukuoka, Japan

Fig. 111. Attractive deck using multiple lengths

On a trade mission to Japan I saw the Marinoa project, a marina, fun park, and shopping centre in Fukuoka. It had a number of timber decks and was the largest decking project in the Fukuoka region. The beauty of the marina deck is exceptional.

The timber species used on the waterfront deck was not known to me but was of a high grade. As a supplier, what stood out to me was the architect's careful use of a spread of lengths, four are used, none over 3.6m long. This is in keeping with our recommendation of designing where the joins are placed and not using lineal decking. This is a wise use of the resource. Unfortunately the deck also included the normal problems of deck design. These were screws in a straight line, joining on a single joist, deterioration of the joist due to fasteners and no dampcourse. This was almost an outstanding deck but its life expectancy has been compromised.

The decks around the remainder of the complex were in jarrah, some of which was of poor quality. I met the supplier who advised it was in fact B grade jarrah. He told me that the grading was questioned at the time but insisted upon by the architect. The normal problems of design and construction were observed. Much of the timber where people frequently walked was under cover but there were large areas that would have been very slippery when wet. We would consider placing the reeds up to be laying decking upside down. When wet, there is little slip resistance when walking along the boards. The natural feature

Fig. 112. B grade jarrah decking laid upside down with screws in straight alignment

may have been more of an issue here as I have observed people in Japan frequently walking in their socks.

Despite sending many containers of spotted gum to Japan we found it impossible to introduce the design practices shown in this guide. This was a pity as the architecture was always extraordinary but let down by a lack of knowledge of detailing and an unwillingness to modify drawings. Our distributor explained that to change a drawing would cause the architect to "lose face". By contrast I have found that generally Australian professionals I have dealt with have been willing to make variations if it meant bringing their client a better project.

Dubai Yacht Club

Fig. 113. Main deck at yacht club

Fig. 114. Newer deck at yacht club

The Dubai Yacht Club deck is included in these case histories because it teaches a valuable lesson. It demonstrates what you "can get away with" in a dry environment. Very importantly, the overall effect of the decks is excellent, and in a country where you do not see much timber the effect is even stronger.

Fig. 115 Small pieces breaking out

Fig. 116. All the decking is 600mm long!

Unquestionably, the detailing is deficient for Australian conditions but generally seems to be working because of the dry conditions. The main deck is laid out in a complex diamond pattern. The small pieces at the points were breaking out creating some trip hazards. Small pieces of timber simply do not work. Using a wider piece would not have helped as it is the screw in the apex that does the damage. The new deck area was made entirely of decking no longer than 600mm! Decking should always extend over a minimum of 3 joists.

Conclusion

When I started specialising in weather exposed timber structures, the guides I found continued to propagate the failed building practices that caused such resistance to timber. It has taken a long time, a lot of money and, I have to admit, my fair share of mistakes to learn what is contained in these pages.

Weather exposed timber structures will test the skill of any professional. I hope that as you have worked through this Guide that you have seen the rewards that can come when you give close attention to the small details of the design. It is not very hard to do, it is all very logical in fact. It really isn't a dark art.

If this Guide helps you, please take the time to write to me and share your images. If you find areas of this Guide that need improvement, or areas that I have missed entirely, please write to me also.

Appendix A. Design Check List

The check list that follows in Table 4 is intended to draw the designer's attention to common shortcomings. It is not intended to meet every design situation.

Foundation Piers, Posts and Abutments	
What are my Design loads?	
Distributed load (5 kPa suggested)	
Point load (4.5 kN suggested)	
Is this structure going to go under water?	
No.	
Yes. At what speed? [Note 1]	
Don't know. Why not? [Note 1]	
For assistance refer to "Site Survey" in my *Light Bridge Manual*	
Have I undertaken a geotechnical investigation?	
No. [Note 1]	
Yes.	
Have I used Galvanised Steel for posts?	
Yes. I have countered ground line corrosion by? [Note 2]	
No.	
Have I used Timber?	
No.	
Yes.	
Am I using round timber with a sapwood envelope?	
Yes.	
No. I will achieve the same design life by?	
Have I set hardwood posts in concrete?	
No	
Yes – why?	
Do circumstances warrant increasing the post size?	
Yes.	
No.	
For assistance look at "Installation of Bollards" in my *Bollard, Traffic Control and Fencing Guide*	
How have I controlled differential movement between deck and path?	
I have done this by?	

I have not thought about it.	
How have I detailed concrete terminations?	
Is timber a minimum 200mm above ground?	
Yes.	
No. How have I ensured durability?	
Water drains forward from back of pad?	
Yes.	
No. Why not?	
Is timber approx 50 mm above pad?	
Yes	
No – Why not?	
Timber and Fasteners for Subframe	
Are most of my sizes 150x75 mm or less?	
Yes.	
No. Why? Have I checked for **ease** of supply? Note 2	
Are my joists 75 mm wide?	
Yes.	
No. How will I stop them splitting?	
How have I specified natural durability?	
Joistwood by OSA or its licensees	
Specified royal species only	
I have just said something meaningless like Dur. 2	
How have I attached the joists to the bearer?	
Triple grips – How will the joists be straightened?	
Bolts	
Brackets – Will they allow straightening?	
Have I needlessly checked into posts?	
Yes	
No	
Have I specified that the joists are to have CN Oil?	
Yes.	
No. Why not?	
Have I ensured the supply without heart in? Note 3	
Yes.	
No.	
Have I specified a Dampcourse?	
Yes. Which one?	
No. Why not?	
How have I ensured there are no oversize holes (even 1 mm) through the dampcourse.	
Have I specified CN emulsion on top of dampcourse	

Yes (Consider using above and below)	
No – why not?	
Have I mentioned not to apply it 6mm thick on hardwood	
Have I specified CN emulsion to cut ends?	
Yes.	
No. Why not? E.g. Check compatibility with paint	
Have I included a diagram showing where to apply finishes?	
Are my fasteners stainless?	
Yes.	
No. Why not	
For assistance refer to "Galvanised or Stainless Fasteners and Connectors" in my book Timber Joints. A true 304 grade is adequate and desirable in screws.	
Have I overspecified treatment?	
No. I have only asked for H3	
Yes. I have asked for the unachievable H4 and H5	
For assistance refer to my *Timber Preservation Guide* where the impossibility of preserving to high levels is explained along with the need to rely on natural durability.	
Decking and Hardware	
How have I ensured the durability of decking?	
Specified Deckwood by OSA or its licencees.	
Specified royal species – no blackbutt.	
I have said something meaningless e.g. F14, Dur. 2.	
Have I specified the sapwood be treated	
H3?	
H4?	
For H4 have I specified independent verification	
How have I ensured an almost clear face?	
Specified Deckwood by OSA or its licensees.	
Specified Structural Grade 1 Face.	
I have said something meaningless like F17.	
For assistance refer to my guide *Grading Hardwood, Understanding 2082*	
How have I gained sufficient slip resistance	
Have I specified a rough sawn face?	
If not, why not?	
Have I specified a film finish?	
Why?	
I have thought through implications of lower slip	

resistance and longevity	
For assistance refer to Wood Solutions technical guide No. 48 Slip Resistance and Wood Pedestrian Surfaces	
How have I ensured conformance to grade?	
I have ensured genuine Deckwood is supplied.	
I require independent grading of alternative decking.	
I haven't, I am trusting the lowest priced tenderer.	
How have I controlled cupping?	
I have used OSA Deckwood.	
I have not made an attempt, ratio exceeds 3.5:1.	
Have I kept the lengths in the ideal range?	
Yes.	
No. Why not?	
Have I set out for set lengths?	
Yes.	
No. Why not?	
Have I determined in there will be any small pieces (Note applies to irregularly shaped decks only)	
I have avoided small pieces of decking by	
Have I specified stainless screws?	
Yes. What grade 304 is suitable (reputable brand only)	
No. Why not?	
Have I included a drawing with screw positions?	
Yes	
No – why not?	
Have I specified fully predrilling?	
Yes.	
No. Why not?	
Have I required inspection of pre-drilling	
What is my target gap?	
? mm	
How I will achieve this?	
Will the micro environment affect the gap?	
How am I changing direction?	
Tapers – how have I controlled small ends (60 mm)?	
Specified OSA or its licensees' standard tapers.	
Other	
Note suits 13 degrees change of direction	
Mitres – How have I controlled pointed ends?	
I have included a drawing showing details.	
I have not controlled the ends.	

I have used a trimmer?	
Yes.	
No. How will you achieve neatness?	
Have I checked consequence of radius adopted?	
How have I addressed shelling out?	
Used Deckwood to minimise likelihood.	
Incorporated a maintenance regime from new.	
Require a six-month inspection and replacement.	
I have ignored this.	
I have required a 5% overorder of decking for maintenance	
Have I checked correct use of CN oil/emulsion?	
Yes.	
No.	
Handrail	
Functional matters	
Pedestrian only and to comply with BCA	
Pedestrian only and to comply with AS5100	
Disabled handrail required	
Bikeway access required	
Minimum height 1.3m	
Have I included an offset rail? Yes/No	
Handrail timber	
Do I have a specific handrail specification	
I have just said something meaningless in this application like F17.	
Have I avoided single span lengths	
Does the profile shed moisture	
Have I trapped moisture	
Have I included volute washers on the posts for shrinkage, Yes/No?	
Are all fastenings horizontal or from underneath, Yes/No?	
Is any timber painted, Yes/No?	
Do I have a site-specific specification Yes/No	
Are paint quality inspections included in specification, Yes/No	
For assistance refer to my guide *Grading Hardwood, Understanding 2082*	
Metal components	
Is any steel fabrication 316 stainless Yes/No	
If No, why not	
Is any steel painted Yes/No?	

Do I have a site-specific specification Yes/No	
Are paint quality inspections included in specification, Yes/No	
Do I have tamper resistant fittings to stainless wire	
Have I fully detailed terminations, etc	
Fire	
Have I avoided the use of sawn CCA treated timber Yes/No?	
Have I considered fire protection to CCA round timber Yes/No?	
Have I specified the use of hardwood that is bushfire resistant Yes/No?	
Table 4. Design check list	

Note 1. If you are serious about this structure and minimising the price of the structure to your client you must have values here. Every assumption that the tenderer has to make will be on the conservative side and your client in the end does not avoid the associated costs. Without a firm answer here your client can be charged substantially more if actual conditions exceed the assumptions stated in the successful tenderer's quotation.

Note 2. This could be caused by either specifying too low an F rating or requiring too little deflection.

Note 3. Not possible with large sizes such as 200x200. Avoid using 150x150 as this is usually heart in material.

Appendix B. Analysis of Alternate Decking material

Guest Contributor Ralph Bailey

When operating Outdoor Structures Australia I was fortunate to have dealings with some remarkable people. I was even more fortunate for some of these supplier/customer relationships to evolve into continuing friendships. One of these is with Ralph Bailey, who along with Tim Guymer were the founders of a leading firm of Brisbane Architects, Guymer Bailey Architects. Ralph and I share a passion for doing things well.

During Christmas 2012, Ralph observed a deck with plastic decking that was not performing well. Many designers are adopting plastic and other alternatives as they are trying to avoid the well known problems of timber decking. In so doing they take on a completely different set of problems. These are problems they are generally not aware of. In an attempt to assist professional designers Ralph kindly agreed to write his observations on hardwood decking and the alternatives. This discussion is not saying - do not use plastic, rather make an informed choice.

REAL TIMBER DECKING OR SYNTHETIC TIMBER DECKING

The verandahs, decks and steps on the Australian home have traditionally been constructed with shot edge or bull nosed boarding of hardwoods of durability Class 1 for the structural members and decking, especially in roofed verandah situations, durability of the verandahs has been excellent as evidenced in the traditional Queensland home. Some of the timbers used were Ironbark, Satinay, Turpentine, Tallowood to name a few.

In recent times hardwood has become harder to source and more expensive. Hardwood species of less durability and possible younger trees are now being used. Often decks and boardwalks are fully exposed to the weather i.e. not roofed. Construction methods and materials are not always appropriate for the situation and verandah and deck failures (in full or part) due to rot are not uncommon. Also quality of workmanship has deteriorated in some circumstances.

With issues of sustainability rightly being pursued by architects, designers and builders in recent times, the option of using one of the many synthetic timber decking products is more frequently being exercised.

Investigation of some of these synthetic timber products has led to a questioning of the sense in using these products.

Some observations on these products include:
- Sagging between joists
- Cracking at fixings

- Very hot to walk or lie on especially dark brown colours
- Fading
- Can be permanently scratched by dragging furniture or other heavy items across it without lifting. Re-sanding is not an option
- "tracking" wear in heavy use zones
- Questionable for use with commercial loadings i.e. bridges & boardwalks
- What do you do with offcuts? Landfill? Burn them?
- What will long term durability be like? How will it fail in the long term? Go brittle and crack and break, erode or soften?

There are numerous brands of synthetic timber being offered to the market and they vary in composition i.e. some have ground up hardwood particles mixed in, others use rice husks and recycled milk bottles and babies nappies, etc. The manufacturers offer various colours and even imitation wood grain texture and all of them push that synthetic wood is a sustainable alternative to real timber decking.

It is interesting also that prefinished bamboo tongue and groove flooring is being promoted as a sustainable option to hardwood tongue and groove flooring. In regard to this bamboo product, one would need to be sure the laminated bamboo pieces in their resin (plastic) embedment have come from renewable bamboo groves and that the user understands exactly what the resin and prefinished components are and can justify shipping container loads of this flooring travelling around the globe if local hardwood can do the job. The other question is also what do you do with the offcuts? Landfill, burn them? They cannot breakdown and return naturally to the soil as will all the offcuts, sanding, waste, etc, of the natural hardwood tongue and groove flooring and decking. This latter objection is also applicable to the synthetic timber decking.

In discussions on the use of real wood versus synthetic wood we should state that all real wood used in construction ideally would be certified by the Forest Stewardship Council or its Australian equivalent – not always possible however at this time.

It is worth listing some of the pros and cons of real wood versus synthetic wood.

Real Wood

FOR	AGAINST
- Real with a natural warmth	- Some hardwoods can be quite expensive
- Pleasant odour	- Unmaintained wood can split, crack and will fade to a grey colour.
- Aesthetically pleasing appearance, especially hardwood	- Rot can be an issue if poorly specified and detailed.
- Some pressure treated softwood decking can be quite inexpensive and is usually readily available (CCA pressure treatment has been discontinued in favour of arsenic-free alternatives)	- Availability and price depends on source and region
	- Certification of source needs to be documented
- Not unreasonably hot to walk on	- Pressure treated softwoods dent and

- barefoot
- Hardwood offcuts can be safely disposed of in landfill to rot or be consumed by termites
- Hardwood can be safely burnt

damage easily. They can warp or bend and contain chemical preservatives that may leak out
- Pressure treated offcuts should not be burnt or put in landfill

Synthetic Wood, Composite Wood, Plastic Wood

FOR
- Less expensive than real wood?
- Weather resistant
- Some are stain resistant
- Some are light weight
- Won't splinter or rot
- Said to be low maintenance i.e. no staining or re-oiling required
- Some have integral colour
- Claimed to be eco, sustainable due to recycled component materials
- Claimed to be easily cleaned with hose or mop

AGAINST
- Some look obviously fake or cheap i.e. texture and/or colour doesn't really resemble wood
- Some are slippery when wet
- Some are not resistant to mould or mildew especially in the shade
- Some will show signs of age and wear/decay/fade
- Some tend to sag and bend more than real wood
- Dark colours very hot to walk on barefoot
- Some will require more substructure than real wood decking
- Expansion/contraction is a problem so special fixings are provided. Direct fixing through the boards is not successful as boards can crack at the fixings
- How do you dispose of off cuts? Burn? Toxic? Landfill?

Aluminium Decking

FOR
- Tough and strong
- Slip resistant if surface textured finish used
- Anodised colour or clear anodised does not fade
- Will not stain
- Can be totally maintenance-free if properly specified and installation is appropriate
- Stays cool under barefoot
- Won't rot, split, splinter or warp
- Fireproof
- Off cuts recyclable to new aluminium products
- Does not try to resemble wood decking unless painted with fake wood grain

AGAINST
- Most expensive decking material
- Can be slippery when wet if texture unidirectional
- The correct aluminium alloy for decking and fixings must be used or corrosion can occur

An architect would choose to use real hardwood for decks, verandahs and boardwalks rather than synthetic imitation wood and accepts that the design and detailing of the installation, the selection of the correct timber species and strength characteristics need to be properly assessed and a maintenance regime established so that the long term performance is not compromised.

The matter of using synthetic timber as a lookalike for real timber decking raises the question of whether these manufacturers might be better to produce a decking product that has its own identity and look, just as aluminium decking has done and has found a place as decking for fire lookout towers or elevated rainforest walks or coastal verandahs, etc.

The decision to use synthetic timber for decking, etc, in lieu of real timber is perhaps based on ready availability, less maintenance and hype at the moment more than price.

Appendix C. A Suitable Decking Specification

The following specification is used in conjunction with tapered sides and a profiled underside to produce Deckwood. Designers should not accept F14, or F17 with species mixes that include blackbutt. I have directly copied a specification from a large council that is written in such a way as to receive our Deckwood or a true equivalent for their bridges. Remember that Deckwood is not just a piece of timber, it is a whole system of building which this specification reflects.

1.00 Seasoned or Un-Seasoned?

Where timber planks are to be fixed directly to steel, Kiln Dried timber is required. This will be 136mm x 42mm F22 Top Un-Seasoned Grade or better Ex. 150 x 50 off saw. Where timber joists are incorporated so we can fix the planks to timber to timber 145mm x 45mm Un-Seasoned F22 Top Grade or better shall be used.

2.00 Fixings

For Timber to Steel use the Simpson Strong-Tie TBG Series to suit the plank and underlying steel joist thickness or similar approved by the Designer, BCW and CA For Timber to Timber use 14 gauge, type 17 with a countersunk/bugle head and a recessed hexagonal drive.

- All screws to be stainless steel, Grade 304.
- All screw holes to be pre-drilled with an appropriate bit combined with a countersink.
- Minimum screw length 75mm for 35 thick decking and 85mm for 45 thick.
- All deck fixings staggered with edge, end and spacings in accordance with AS1720
- Minimum Joist width 75mm.
- All bolts for Timber Joists etc to Structural Steel or Timber joist to Timber Bearer etc. to be Min M12 316 Stainless Steel threaded rod with Glenlock nut and washer top and bottom.
- Timber joist tops should be coated with CN emulsion to counter the effects of water held at the joist-deck interface by capillary forces.
- In addition a Malthoid damp proof course (DPC) shall be laid along the joist-top protects the member from degrade. The Malthoid should be coated with a CN emulsion preservative paste to counter the effects of water held at the joist-deck interface by capillary forces.
- For steel joists Denso tape in place of the CN emulsion and Malthoid.

3.00 Species

Timber shall be selected from the following species:-
- spotted gum
- tallowwood
- ironbark.

4.00 Timber Quality

Timber will be graded under a hardwood quality control programme conforming to ISO 9002. At the time of grading, the bottom and sides of the plank will conform to AS 2082, Structural Grade No 2 while the exposed sawn (upper) face surface shall be free of:
- Loose and unsound knots

- Shakes
- Loose gum veins
- Knot holes
- Termite galleries
- Want, wane and bark
- Checks wider than 1mm
- End splits wider than 1mm
- Included bark
- Borer holes larger than 3mm diameter
- In addition, permitted defects will not cover more that 15% of the top face.
- Permissible defects on the upper face may include 1 only borer hole up to 6mm diameter per plank.

5.00 Preservative Treatment

Treatment, natural durability classes and combinations will conform to AS 1604, TUMA (Timber Utilization and Marketing Act Qld 1987) and TMA (Timber Marketing Act NSW 1977). Sapwood will be treated to Level H3 in accordance with TUMA. A certificate of treatment will be provided.

6.00 Tolerances

The actual cross-sectional dimensions of timber at the time of processing shall not vary from the dimensions stated by more that the following:-

- width 3 mm
- thickness 0, +2 mm
- length 0 mm
- length (cut to size) 5 mm

Length	Maximum Bow	
	35mm	45mm
1800	10	10
2400	20	15
3600	50	35
4800	70	50

Length	Maximum spring(mm)			
	70 wide	90 wide	120 wide	145 wide
1800	7	5	4	3
2400	12	10	7	6
3600	25	20	15	13
4800	30	30	30	25

7.00 Surface Finish

Gauged on the bottom with the sound sawn face being exposed uppermost.

Timber to be coated with Lanotec, Tanacoat or similar subject to BCW confirming for CA approval the product's suitability after performance testing and establishing possible environmental impact, sustain ability and checking availability and lead times etc.

8.00 Laying

Lay the unseasoned timber edge face to edge face, and the kiln dried with a 3mm gap.

9.00 Contract

Allow 3 month lead time for Kiln Dried Timber

www.ingramcontent.com/pod-product-compliance
Lightning Source LLC
Chambersburg PA
CBHW041519220426
43667CB00002B/35